Cre

Create or Die

Essays on the Artistry of Dennis Hopper

Stephen Lee Naish

Amsterdam University Press

Cover illustration: unknown / mptvimages.com

Cover design: Kok Korpershoek, Amsterdam
Lay-out: Crius Group, Hulshout

Amsterdam University Press English-language titles are distributed in the US and Canada by the University of Chicago Press.

ISBN 978 90 8964 858 7
e-ISBN 978 90 4852 713 7
DOI 10.5117/9789089648587
NUR 670

For J&H

Contents

Introduction

Let us consider two important factors, the two poles of the creation of art: the artist on the one hand, and on the other the spectator who later becomes the posterity.[1]

– Marcel Duchamp

The career of Dennis Hopper was haunted by a single, persistent spectre—that of Frank Booth. Hopper's career and even certain extremes of his life could be seen as a lifetime preparation towards playing Frank Booth, the sadistic menace in director David Lynch's dark and disturbing *Blue Velvet* (1986). As we shall see throughout this text, Hopper's performances as damaged, deranged, and alienated characters range as far back as *Night Tide* (1961) and continued up until *The River's Edge* (1986). The darkness sometimes lay beneath the surface but was persistently present. In Frank Booth, Hopper found the channel for all his previous characters' rage and alienation. Subsequently, Frank Booth and his exuberant mannerisms would go on to define Hopper's career post-*Blue Velvet*. The frailties and subtleties of Hopper's pre-*Blue Velvet* characters were overwhelmed by the Booth-like bluster. The performances in films such as *Red Rock West* (1991), *Super Mario Bros* (1993), and *Speed* (1994) rely heavily on intimidation and menace to communicate their anger towards the world.

My own fascination with the life and work of Dennis Hopper began many years ago during a late night television screening of *Blue Velvet*. Through a fog of lethargy and a half-drunk bottle of red wine, I was drawn into the opening sequence of white picket fences, cloudless blue skies, and immaculate green lawns. Bobby Vinton's woozy 1963 hit 'Blue Velvet' drifted in over the opening images, cosy and hypnotic. A firefighter waves to the camera as he slowly passes by on his red fire truck through the leafy streets of an American suburb. An old man waters his freshly cut lawn, his little dog snoops around the bushes. I was made to feel relatively at ease with the peaceful scene that was unfolding. Suddenly the old man drops to the ground, grasping at his neck in agony. The hose shoots clear water towards the blue sky, which in turn attracts the little dog to lap it up. Then the camera, and also the audience, descends beneath the lawn. Below ground, the insects crawl and scramble over each other in a grotesque close up. The sound of the insects heaving was reminiscent of a thunderous machine. *Blue Velvet* was a film where nothing was what it seemed. Darkness lay beneath the sheen. Our descent beneath the layer of innocence takes us into a wicked world.

It was past midnight when Dennis Hopper, as the perverted small-time gangster Frank Booth, makes his first appearance. Frank charges into the dimly lit and sparsely furnished apartment of Dorothy Vallens (Isabella Rossellini), fidgeting uncontrollably and apprehensively turning his head in every direction. A wild animal scoping out his domain. We know nothing of Frank or Dorothy's relationship, but it soon becomes apparent that Frank has a mental and psychical hold over her. He settles for a moment, coolly takes a swig of bourbon from a glass, watching his victim in torment. Frank demands that Dorothy spread her legs. When Frank first bursts onto the screen, my stomach fluttered nervously, an anxiety descended: something terrible was about to happen, and I was proven right. The scene gave the impression of a humming electric current running below the surface, but moments later, it exploded into an all-out shock. Frank Booth inhales from his cylinder of mysterious gas (nitrous oxide/amyl nitrate, depending on which source you believe) that he has concealed inside his leather jacket, and turns brutal. Frank snarls and moans whilst he violently rapes Dorothy. It was then, and still is, a deeply shocking piece of cinema. The camera is kept at an almost constant distance from the action, as in the perspective of the film's young protagonist Jeffrey Beaumont (Kyle MacLachlan), who helplessly watches the scene unfold through the gaps in Dorothy's closet. David Lynch's directing turns his audience into a voyeur of a sick game. We observe Dorothy's torment in unnerving realism. Moreover, as tensions continue to climb and Frank 'climaxes' (we are never sure if this is an external or internal release; for one thing, Frank does not remove his pants), the audience is further transformed from voyeur to guilty party, an unwitting accomplice to an awful crime. Like Jeffrey watching from the closet, the audience is unable and unwilling to intervene.

Although a creation of David Lynch, credit for the ferocious Frank Booth must go to Dennis Hopper. In Frank Booth, Hopper created one of the most merciless cinema villains. Conversely, Frank's inability to control his impulses makes the audience feel just a little sympathetic towards him. Charles Drazen, in his book *On Blue Velvet,* described these feelings towards Frank Booth accordingly: "I have to confess that, having watched *Blue Velvet* many times now, I've grown rather fond of him…I no longer think of Frank as evil. In the grip of evil maybe, but, therefore, to be pitied".[2] I share Drazen's viewpoint. Frank Booth does indeed deserve some sympathy for the horrors he must have witnessed and experienced to make him the monster he becomes. Drazen's point is well made in regards to Frank Booth, but this could also be applied to many of Hopper's characters who suffer from the same affliction. As will become apparent in this text, Hopper's characters are a line-up of misfits that often arouse our pity for one reason or another.

After the scene above concluded, my heart returned to its usual pace. The film continued. Of course, the calm was not to last. Frank Booth re-emerged later as a jabbering bully, a sadistic freak, smearing red lipstick over his face and taunting Jeffery Beaumont with violent and, one might read, sexual menace (Booth smears red lipstick on Beaumont and compliments him with "pretty pretty"). In his enthralling still-frame analysis of *Blue Velvet,* writer Nicholas Rombes comments that "Frank seems so otherworldly, so schizophrenically disjointed from natural time, so uniquely characterised as someone (or *thing*) from another place entirely."[3] This is certainly true of Frank Booth, whose imposition in *Blue Velvet*'s dream-like calm is unnerving. As with Drazen's viewpoint, Rombes' analysis of Frank's incoherence within *Blue Velvet* could also relate to many of Hopper's characters. His appearance in numerous films triggers a dislocation from the context of the given film. One of the aims of this text is to explore this destabilising facet of Hopper's career in film and reality; to make a case for this "otherworldly" premise as one that is deliberate on the part of Hopper. His approach in countless films often sees him jump from the screen, shooting out wild stares, uttering random and improvised gibberish, whether the scene calls for such action or not. Whilst in other films, he remains in the background, allowing his co-stars an opportunity in the spotlight and acting as a soundboard for them to improvise and attempt new approaches. In both respects, Hopper still becomes the centre of awareness and the crucial pivot of the film's trajectory. In a retrospective article in *Film Comment,* Howard Hampton sums this up as "…oscillating between put-on and implosion" and an "acute consciousness of camera and audience: he wouldn't necessarily act with his fellow actors so much as *at* them."[4] Hopper was well aware of his own on-screen and off-screen persona, and he employed this awareness throughout his career.

Blue Velvet had me hooked. Dennis Hopper's seminal 1969 film *Easy Rider,* which he co-wrote, directed, and starred in, had already become a personal favourite. *Easy Rider* acted like a springboard towards the discovery of the New Hollywood movement of the 1960s and 1970s and its aesthetic qualities. I obsessively tracked down more and more of Hopper's films from a collection of movies that cover six decades of acting and directorial work. From taking an interest in his film work, I also became fascinated with the other aspects of his career and rollercoaster life. From as early as the mid-1950s, Hopper had been a passionate artist and photographer and continued to be involved in the ever-blossoming art scene of Los Angeles as an art collector and connoisseur (see the 2008 documentary *The Cool School* for an in-depth interview with Hopper regarding this aspect of his life). His knowledge of art was renowned and encyclopedic, and he could often be spotted at the gallery openings of well-established artists and debut shows from young and emerging artists alike. Notorious accounts of his overenthusiastic consumption of drugs and booze have filled chapters of books, from biographies of those who encountered and worked alongside him to exposés on the New Hollywood movement of the late 1960s and early 1970s (tales of which can be found in Peter Fonda's 1998 memoir *Don't Tell Dad* and Peter Biskind's 1999 New Hollywood exposé *Easy Riders, Raging Bulls*). Dennis Hopper's film career was many things: stalled and uncertain at times, fuelled by bouts of genius and extraordinary egotism, in some sense his talent was wasted by copious amounts of drugs, ego, and madness. But if his life is taken as a transcendent, artistic statement of triumph and failure, then one could argue, as Petra Gilroy-Hirtz does in the monograph *The Lost Album* (2012), that within Hopper's life "There was no normalcy, no boredom, no taboos."[5] A life lived to creative fruition.

In this text, I endeavour to uncover Dennis Hopper's importance within popular culture. Obviously as Hopper was an American actor, his importance was mainly confined to American shores, but there are moments when we reach further afield. The first essay, 'Scenes from a Revolutionary Life', looks at Hopper's film work in a chronological, decade-by-decade account. By placing his most critically acclaimed and commercially successful roles side by side with some lesser known film performances, I attempt to offer an understanding of Hopper's role within cinema and popular culture. In the second essay, 'Hip-Hopp: Dennis Hopper and Music', I look at the inspiration he took from popular music to soundtrack his directorial films. I also examine the role he played in the advancement of music videos, MTV, and live musical performance. This essay is also an opportunity to explore Hopper's influence on modern music—from folk and punk to hip-hop. The third essay, 'The Elephant in the Room: Dennis Hopper and American Politics', is about Hopper's life within American left and right-wing politics, which is often reflected in his film roles. In the longer essay, 'Love and Hate: The Conflict of Emotions in *The Blackout* and *Carried Away*', I analyse two very contrasting performances in the two films and explore Hopper's emotional portrayal of love and lust on film. In the essay entitled 'Commercial Breakdown: Dennis Hopper and the World of Advertisements', I look at Hopper's place within print advertisements and televised commercials in America and abroad. In 'White Light/White Heat:

Actor and Character Collide in *White Star*', I study Hopper's excursion into European art house cinema with *White Star* (1984) and his astounding if incredibly raw acting performance in this film, which acts as a reflection of his circumstances at the time the film was made. I then move on to an exploration of Hopper's art and photography, commenting on his evolution as an artist and reflecting on the influence his artistic endeavours have had on his film work. By way of conclusion, the essay 'The Fourth Wall' returns to the subject touched upon in this introduction: Hopper's disjointed and destabilising effect within film, art, and popular culture. His breaking down of the unseen fourth wall—the audience perspective—in which we observe Hopper's self-referral of his own cinematic past and also his off-screen persona.

This text is not a standard review of Dennis Hopper's films. I am not interested in informing a reader if any of Hopper's films are good, bad, or mediocre. If my own personal voice creeps in throughout the text, this is somewhat deliberate. So much has been written of Hopper's work over the decades, yet some of the subjects covered in this text have not been widely considered and so are based on personal analysis combined with other sources. My aim is to create a grander picture of a brilliant if deeply flawed artist, one who lived by the axiom "create or die".

Scenes from a Revolutionary Life

How Dennis Hopper Conquered the American Century

In a 1971 interview with chat show host Merv Griffin, Dennis Hopper, then promoting his second directorial film *The Last Movie,* stated that he saw himself as a social critic and that his films *Easy Rider* and *The Last Movie* commented directly on America's social ills. With the critical backlash of *The Last Movie*, Hopper had become a staunch defender of his own work but also realised his vision was way ahead of the majority of mainstream American film audiences. Towards the end of the interview, Hopper comments that *The Last Movie* is essentially "...a social protest film, and I'm going to go on being a social critic." He goes on to add, "but I'm going to have to simplify and romanticize my work so I can identify with an audience".[1] Dennis Hopper ingrained himself within the very fabric of American popular culture. His continuous social commentary drew into his movies subtle elements of pop culture, music, politics, and his own reality that represented the themes of the era. Consciously or unconsciously, his films and art have acted as reflections of the times in which they were made. In order to understand Hopper's cultural value, we must first take into account his importance in film, the aspect of his career that he is most widely recognised for. What follows below is a chronological exploration and summary of Hopper's film performances that also takes into account his directorial work. I have also summarised the political and social landscapes in which these films were made, in order to better comprehend Hopper's effect on the American psyche. Although some films have been left out from the study for various reasons (1993's *Mario Bros* springs to mind), I have endeavoured to include the films that are significant to Hopper's artistic evolution, the critically acclaimed performances, and those films that have been popular with audiences, either based on commercial success, critical praise, or cult status.

The Matinee Idol and the Method

America enjoyed a glorious renaissance in the post-war boom of the 1950s. After the economic slump of the 1930s, the horrors of the Second World War, and the grim attrition of the Korean War, America was ready to begin again. The inauguration of President Eisenhower in 1953 brought with it a "new optimism and unprecedented prosperity"[2] to American society.

The foundation of the American Dream was being laid in the ownership of automobiles, a house in suburbia, and an abundance of children. Hollywood was still in the grip of producing epic westerns and rousing musical films—until, that is, actors such as Marlon Brando and James Dean, among others, brought a sense of realism and naturalism to cinema, paving the way for the young actors and filmmakers to seize the opportunity of reinventing cinema for themselves and the more youthful audience.

In 1955, an eighteen-year-old Dennis Hopper made his film debut as a thuggish gang member named Goon in the seminal teenage movie *Rebel Without a Cause*. A brief yet memorable performance as an epileptic in the television drama *Medic* (1954-1956) was Hopper's calling card to the Hollywood studios. Hopper's startling intensity and dedication to his craft was spotted as star potential by the studio system. *Rebel Without a Cause* was a vehicle for two of Hollywood's hottest young actors, James Dean and Natalie Wood. Whilst Hopper's role as Goon may not have been significant within the context of the film, the guidance that James Dean offered the young Hopper, and the subsequent friendship that developed between the two, was a lasting influence on the rest of Hopper's film and artistic career. Dean introduced Hopper to method acting, demonstrating to Hopper how it was possible to be in the moment and in the time and space of the character's world. Hopper has often commented on the impact of witnessing James Dean's acting ability and style: "I literally picked him up, threw him into the car and said 'What are you doing? How can I do it? Do I have to go to Strasberg?"[3] Dennis Hopper did go to Strasberg, Lee Strasberg that is, the renowned acting tutor who was based at The Actors Studio in New York City. Strasberg adapted the acting philosophy of Russian theatre director and actor Constantin Stanislavski into that of 'The Method'. Strasberg coached the likes of Paul Newman, Marlon Brando, Dustin Hoffman, Ben Gazzara, and Marilyn Monroe, among many others in method acting. Hopper was taught that the method approach of acting—as described by Stanislavski in his seminal text, *An Actor Prepares*—was not to "present merely the external life of his character. He must fit his own human qualities to the life of this person, and pour into it all of his own soul."[4] In effect, the actor has to exist as the character and improvise the real-life, day-to-day ticks the character may comprise, using experience and memories related to the actor's own life to feed that of the character's life. As Strasberg himself relates: "The extraordinary thing about acting is that life itself is actually used to create artistic results...The actor uses real sensation and real behavior. That actual reality is the material of our craft."[5] This is vital to understanding Hopper's acting technique, as his life and film performance have often bled into one another, as we'll see later when the film *White Star* is discussed. Audiences would never see James Dean's full potential realised. A high-speed car crash on September 30th, 1955 robbed the world of an iconic star and immortalised Dean forever as a rebellious and defiant teenager. Deeply troubled by the loss of his friend, Hopper inherited the artistic career of which Dean was cheated.

Hopper continued to adhere to the method approach, even within a standard Hollywood production. For example, in *Giant* (1955), the epic movie directed by George Stevens, Hopper and Dean provided offbeat performances within the setting of a standard Texan oil melodrama. The film's grandeur is typical of the Hollywood epics of the 1950s but also contains some elements of a "...critique and a bit of a satire of Texas materialism, anti-intellectualism, machismo, and racism."[6] *Giant* was literally giant, clocking in at an epic 201 minutes running time. The film graciously tells its weaving story spanning decades. In a review for the reissued and restored DVD version, James Berardinelli makes an interesting point about how "...although *Giant* may not be a classic in the purest sense of the word, it's a fine example of a virtually extinct genre".[7] It is fitting that the genre of the extravagant Hollywood epic, of which *Giant* is a prime example, was to be essentially killed off by the likes of Dennis Hopper and the New Hollywood directors a decade later. The young breed, bored and disillusioned with the bloated studio star system, eventually invented their own means of creativity and made opportunities for themselves. However, for now the studios were still in the hands of the moguls and the dictatorial producers and directors.

The remainder of the 1950s and early 1960s were something of a professional washout for Hopper. He became blacklisted from the studio system, having earned himself a reputation for being too difficult to direct. His confrontation with director Henry Hathaway on the set of the Western standard *From Hell to Texas* (1958) over the delivery of a line of dialogue became something of legend and a staple anecdote in almost all of Hopper's subsequent interviews. The film itself is a classic of the Western genre. It is, however, interesting to understand Hathaway's influence on his young nemesis. In a 1986 interview with *Film Comment*, Hopper stated, "Hathaway changed my life a lot...And I learned a lot from him."[8] Hopper, after all, went on to direct a revisionist Western of sorts with *Easy Rider*, replacing the chivalrous steeds with roaring motorcycles, and his second film *The Last Movie* featured a standard Western 'movie within a movie' production. Hathaway would ultimately bury the hatchet with Hopper in the mid-1960s, inviting him to appear in *The Sons of Katie Elder* (1965) and *True Grit* (1969), both of which starred John Wayne. Nevertheless, Hopper's vision of his artistic future was certain. Hopper took a different road to that which was offered to him by the studio system, starting a journey towards a much more authentic, artistic, and independent calling.

The Counterculture Icon and the Invention of New Hollywood

The 1960s brought to America, and in some respects the Western world, a revolution of free love and a never-ending summer of drugs, sex, and happiness, at least on the surface. In reality, the decade itself was a complex game of peace and war, life and death, hope and hopelessness. The Age of Aquarius was drowned out by the assassinations of President John F. Kennedy in 1963, his younger brother Robert F. Kennedy, and civil rights activist Martin Luther King Jr., both killed in 1968. In 1962, the nuclear posturing of the Soviet Union and America led to the Cuban Missile Crisis, which nearly turned the Cold War between America and the Soviet Union into a very heated conflict. As writer Jenny Diski described it in her 2009 memoir *The 1960s*: "the peaceful world... on the verge of exploding into the worst and final conflict".[9] That same year, American involvement in the Vietnam War escalated, with uncensored images of graphic warfare beaming into the homes of Americans via the nightly news broadcast. The war was described as an "enterprise of noble ideals and impulses", as Robert Manning puts it in his preface to *The Vietnam Experience: Images of War*, "...but like some prehistoric monster lumbering blindly into the asphalt swamp, descended into tragedy."[10] Socially, however, the decade made better progress. After a citizen-led political upheaval, civil rights, gay rights, and women's rights began to be seriously addressed. The decade is fondly remembered for the change in perspective, but more realistically it was a decade of resistance. Hopper sums up the decade best in an interview with Matthieu Orléan, in which he states that "the country was falling apart: the Vietnam War, the Black Panthers... It was a difficult time: there were riots in every city in the United States."[11] Hopper's reflection here is perhaps more valid than the nostalgically rosy view of the 1960s. Certainly Hopper's directorial debut *Easy Rider* would comment more negatively on the decade, but there was social commentary to be made in many of the films Hopper appeared in as an actor prior to *Easy Rider.*

Dennis Hopper spent much of the 1960s appearing in small, independently made films. The most notable was experimental filmmaker Curtis Harrington's *Night Tide*, an "arthouse film in the French tradition made by an underground artist"[12] which cast Hopper in the lead role as Johnny Drake, a young sailor who becomes infatuated with a woman called Mora, who believes she is a mermaid. Hopper played the role with a quiet awkwardness and underlying paranoia, a side to his acting repertoire that would be virtually forgotten in subsequent decades. On the DVD commentary with Harrington, Hopper stated that *Night Tide* was possibly the first feature to be made outside of the traditional studio system and also to be shot on the streets, instead of on a soundstage setting.[13] This guerrilla filmmaking approach by Harrington would become an important aspect of Hopper's own directorial methodology of taking the cameras out of the soundstages into the streets.

Writer and director Roger Corman's American Independent Pictures (AIP) also played a huge role in shaping Hopper and the New Hollywood aesthetic towards low-budget, independent filmmaking. AIP's focus was the youth market and especially the drive-in feature that exploited controversial aspects of American culture: topics such as drugs, sex, and the subcultures of motorcycle gangs and surfing. Most notably, AIP focused on the notorious biker gang The Hell's Angels, whose chapters swept across America during the post-war years. The three future stars of *Easy Rider* all appeared in exploitation biker films. Hopper appeared as gang leader Chino in *The Glory Stompers* (1967), whilst Peter Fonda starred in the more successful *The Wild Angels* (1967) alongside Nancy Sinatra. Both films were made by AIP. Jack Nicholson appeared as a young gas stop attendant called Poet, who is entangled in the exploits of a violent biker gang in *Hells Angels on Wheels* (1967). Not dissimilar to the plot and narratives of many other biker films of the era, *The Glory Stompers* does feature an at times out of sync performance from Hopper. Film director Quentin Tarrantino pointed this out in an interview with Hopper: "...it looks like you're improvising it throughout the whole thing...when you're fighting this guy, you beat him up, and then you look around and say 'Anybody else got anything to say? Turn it on, man, just turn it on.'"[14] This continued improvisation by Hopper led the infuriated director of *The Glory Stompers*, Anthony M. Lanza, to abandon the picture midway through filming, leaving Hopper to pick up the directorial reins for the remainder of the shoot. Hopper went without credit for his first directorial work, yet his prints can be spotted in the film's "picturesque long shots of bikers riding over sand dunes and on a highway against a reddish setting sun"[15], which could be viewed as a prelude to the iconic cross-country wanderings of *Easy Rider's* long and beautiful wide shots of Billy and Wyatt traversing the rugged landscapes.

Another API production that caused a great deal of controversy at the time and for subsequent decades was *The Trip* (1967). Due to its controversial nature, *The Trip* went unreleased in the United Kingdom until 2004. The film concerns hallucinogenic drugs, in this case LSD, a drug that was becoming commonplace in the last half of the 1960s. The mental effects of LSD were explored to great depth by journalist Tom Wolfe in his book *The Electric Kool-Aid Acid Test* (1968). *The Trip* cast Peter Fonda as Paul Groves, a young director of television advertisements who, wishing to make sense of his drab life, takes a tab of LSD. Hopper was cast in the role of Max, a drug guru who supplies the LSD, and peppers every sentence with "man". The film plays out in vignettes that become wildly more surreal as Paul's trip progresses. Hopper again had a chance to direct the second unit of the shoot and contributed the film's experimental and most naturalistic scenes. Wandering aimlessly through the neon-lit strip of Los Angeles, Fonda's character is bombarded in quick succession with flashing images of advertisements, billboards, motel and store signs, making the scene a companion piece to the graveyard trip in *Easy Rider.* After a decade of playing minor roles in API productions to no real avail, actor Jack Nicholson had turned to script writing. Nicholson wrote the screenplay for *The Trip* and later went on to produce the script for the surrealist/musical film *Head* (1968), a vehicle for pop band The Monkees. The next year, and after a supporting turn in *Easy Rider,* Nicholson would make a grand return to acting in such New Hollywood fare as *Five Easy Pieces* (1970) and turn writer/director for *Drive, He Said* (1971). *The Trip* was an attempt to explore drug culture in a more constructive light. Fonda's character may be on LSD, but he does not kill or molest anyone during his excursion into the city; he is depicted as perplexed by the world but not against it. Hopper's portrayal of the drug dealer Max as a calm and peaceful hippie is also at odds with the general depiction of drug dealers as hard narcotic pushers. This distinction is also made in *Easy Rider,* especially with the inclusion of the song 'The Pusher' by Steppenwolf on the soundtrack. The lyrics state: "You know the dealer / the dealer is a man / With the love grass in his hand / Oh but the pusher is a monster / Good God, he's not a natural man."[16] *The Trip* could also be read as an early indictment of capitalism and commercialism. During his trip, Fonda's character Paul Groves experiences a mock trial, with Hopper's character Max as judge, accusing him of selling out his artistic integrity in order to make a living as a director of television advertisements. Paul's declaration that what he does is "a living" is unconvincing to himself and the audience.

The movie that perfectly crystallised the schism of war and peace in 1960s America was *Easy Rider. Easy Rider* stands as a milestone in American New Wave cinema. It is a monumental little movie that generated enough heat to change the direction of Hollywood, and independent movies alike. *Easy Rider* allowed the New Hollywood ethos to fully mature and for personal auteur movies to be made in the early 1970s, such as Bob Rafelson's *Five Easy Pieces*, Peter Bogdanovich's *The Last Picture Show* (1971), and, of course, Dennis Hopper's own ill-fated *The Last Movie*. *Easy Rider* involves two drifters chasing the American Dream on custom-built motorcycles across the land they call home, the same land that, ironically, does not want them there. The people they meet and the places they travel through define the American 1960s. *Easy Rider* distils sadness, futility, and the improbability of living in a truly free society without ever commenting directly on the grim circumstances the country was facing, such as the Vietnam War, the civil rights movement, and the Cold War. *Easy Rider's* visual beauty and vibrant colour did not portray a country in turmoil, at least on the surface. Underneath the rot was setting in, witnessed by the opposition that Billy and Wyatt encounter on their travels. The film's all-conquering soundtrack, which signalled a new and dynamic approach to movie soundtracks by incorporating already known and popular rock and folk songs, darkens the mood of the film, with songs such as Steppenwolf's grim 'The Pusher' and Bob Dylan's 'It's Alright Ma (I'm only Bleeding)' with its lyrical couplets forewarning doom:

> Pointed threats they bluff with scorn/ Suicide remarks are torn/ from the fool's gold mouthpiece the hollow horn/plays wasted words proves to warn/That he not busy being born/ is busy dying.[17]

Hopper's comprehension of youth culture was clear in his choice of music (more of which later). Every song in some way corresponds with the visual. It is impossible to hear Steppenwolf's 'Born to be Wild' or The Byrds' 'I Wasn't Born to Follow' without envisioning Billy and Wyatt rambling across the American landscape. With all the weight of trying to define an era, it is easy to forget that it is often the campfire interactions of Hopper and Fonda, and later, when they are joined on the road by Jack Nicholson's George Hanson, which really drive the loosely tied plot together. The ad hoc conversations provide some invigorating black humour and insightful, if slightly undeveloped, observations ("I mean, it's real hard to be free when you are bought and sold in the marketplace"). *Easy Rider* could have easily become another exploitation biker movie, which proved so popular during the mid to late 1960s. It is credit to Hopper and Fonda that they saw an opportunity to summarise the era. *Easy Rider* is a movie that plays to a disenfranchised youth, to the kids who at the time of its arrival were the ones who were going to have to clean up the mess in the post-1960s. Following the success of *Easy Rider*, Dennis Hopper and Peter Fonda began to distance themselves, both personally and professionally, from one another. A disagreement with screenwriter Terry Southern and between themselves over the authorship of *Easy Rider* was never fully resolved and fractured the relationship and artistic partnership. Fonda showed up fleetingly in the background of Hopper's *The Last Movie*, but after that film, their on-screen alliance was severed.

The Burn Out and The Vietnam War

The 1970s was the comedown following the highs of the 1960s. America was complicit in an unpopular war in Vietnam, and the idyllic and utopian promises of the 1960s never came to fruition. Race riots, anti-war protests, and the feeling that you'd been swindled from the word go was all that was left. Harsh truths had begun to set in. The promise of offbeat, personal filmmaking that was initiated by the New Hollywood set quickly evaporated (Dennis Hopper was in some ways partially responsible for this, as we shall see). The younger interns of New Hollywood began to break from their masters and introduce a genre of film that pulled audiences into theatres in their millions. Films such as Steven Spielberg's *Jaws* (1975) and *Star Wars* (1977) by George Lucas (who had begun his career under the guidance of Francis Ford Coppola) set the standard for the summer blockbuster movie. The blockbuster genres' release dates became national events, the special effects-laden narratives were pure spectacle; the films became part of huge marketing campaigns that included toys, t-shirts, and fast food tie-ins (the blockbuster phenomenon is explored in British film critic Tom Shone's 2004 book *Blockbuster: How Hollywood Learned to Stop Worrying and Love the Summer*). In order to compete with the blockbusters, cinema began to hark back to the 1940s heyday of grand scale epics but with added visual spectacle. The smaller independent films were drowned out by the bluster of big budget moviemaking. Enormous sums of money began to fund these illustrious projects, leaving little time or money for the smaller, personal film. Nevertheless, the 1970s still managed to produce some of the most outstanding cinema in the form's short history.

Easy Rider made Dennis Hopper and Peter Fonda cultural icons. This meant that they were entrusted with free artistic rein in New Hollywood. Universal Studios were more than happy to supply the then-unprecedented one million dollars and cede complete creative control to each of these lucrative stars for their next projects. Peter Fonda chose to direct and star in *The Hired Hand* (1971), a lyrical, slow-burning revisionist western in which he played a roaming cowboy returning home to his wife after seven years away. Hopper took his million dollars and his entourage of actors, friends, and hangers-on into the high mountains of Peru to make *The Last Movie*, a tale of the adverse effects of an intrusive film production on an indigenous people. Hopper had envisioned the film as being his first directorial work. He and *Rebel Without a Cause* screenwriter Stewart Stern had begun the writing process in the early 1960s. However, the film strayed so far from the original screenplay that Stern felt it was not "... an accurate representation" of his work and that Hopper "didn't use the scenes as they were written in the screenplay and that he chose to improvise with people who were not up to that kind of improvisation, but also that he hadn't shot scenes that were essential."[18] One could argue that Hopper's excess and mythmaking got in the way of producing a straightforward narrative film.

As well as directing *The Last Movie*, Hopper also played the lead role of Kansas, a movie stuntman who stays behind once the production company has left and goes native with the Peruvian villagers. Perceiving some sort of black magic in the movies, the villagers begin to re-enact the pretend violent scenes they have witnessed, with real violent consequences. Both Hopper and Fonda's films—though brave and in some quarters critically acclaimed—were commercial failures. *The Last Movie* won the critics' prize at the 1971 Venice Film Festival, but its original New York screening lasted only two weeks. Hopper's film failed to garner any respectable mainstream press or positive reviews. With the failure of *The Last Movie*, Hopper's desire to make important, socially conscious movies came to an end. He exiled himself in his New Mexico compound and waited for Hollywood to come crawling back for his bankability, or for Hollywood to catch up with his artistic vision. Neither of these things would happen for a very long time. Despite this, *The Last Movie* is clearly an accomplished piece of art cinema. The film flows on a phantasmagoria of sound and images that conjure up a disjointed yet affecting experience. As Andrew Tracy in his critique of the film points out: "The overall effect is to remove the viewer from any kind of perspective perch, to erase the illusion of a guiding viewpoint and a stable base of judgment and force the viewer to confront the film as a persistently confounding object."[19] It is interesting to view the film as per Tracy's description and to take oneself out of the narrative and observe the film as a singular artistic object. *The Last Movie* positions itself as ethnography—a way in which one can study a culture and people by immersion. *The Last Movie* was an example of Hopper's desire to transcend film and art into a immersive and sensory experience. However, the film's title was prophetic, as due to the critical backlash it was to be Hopper's last directorial film for a decade. Yet it was also the first and last of its kind for a long time: an art house film made within the confines of Hollywood's studio system.

As a companion piece to *The Last Movie*, the documentary film *The American Dreamer* (1971) fills in some of the gaps and answers questions as to why Hopper's relatively straightforward screenplay became so distorted. The documentary was directed by Lawrence Schiller and L.M. Kit Carson. Carson would later go on to adapt the screenplay for *Paris, Texas* (1984) and write the original screenplay for *The Texas Chainsaw Massacre 2* (1986), which starred Hopper. The film chronicles the intense post-production of *The Last Movie* whilst also taking time to allow a tripped-out Hopper to theorise about life, film, art, religion, and sex. These stream-of-consciousness mutterings bear some resemblance to the madcap statements made by Hopper's photojournalist character in *Apocalypse Now* seven years later. *The American Dreamer* adds something to the mythical quality that Hopper was attempting to establish around himself. The rambling interviews interspersed with footage of Hopper—bearded and in ragged jeans, gun under arm, walking over windswept landscapes, accompanied by rambling folk songs on the soundtrack—are for the most part evocative of the outlaws and bandits that once roamed the wilderness. The interviews reveal a great deal about Hopper's intentions and obsessions regarding his film and with film itself as an art form. It also demonstrates the many distractions and temptations that Hopper faced in the aftermath of *Easy Rider*'s fame. Drugs, drink, and women begin to pull him away from the task of finishing his film within the given time and budget. One scene in particular is deeply uncomfortable. A group of young girls are bussed in to actively participate in group sex with Hopper. With his manic stare, shaggy beard, long hair, and surrounded by lovelorn females, one cannot help but see visual similarities to cult leader and serial killer Charles Manson. *The American Dreamer* is a shambolic attempt to paint Hopper in the colours of an American folk hero. To be fully understood, it has to be seen alongside *The Last Movie* and in the context of that film's artistic triumphs and commercial failures.

Another companion piece of sorts to *The Last Movie*—though set in the arid outback of Australia as opposed to the rugged mountains of Peru—is *Mad Dog Morgan* (1976). The film shares the mosaic aesthetics of *The Last Movie*, and its production was hampered by Hopper's excessive drinking and substance abuse. Daniel Morgan was an outlaw of Irish descent during the Australian gold rush of the mid-1800s. Morgan was arrested for armed robbery after the goldfield he was mining was raided by a group of racist thugs, unhappy about the presence of Chinese miners. He escaped the raid, but without the most basic supplies for survival, he held up a group of horsemen at gunpoint in order to take their spare clothes and blankets. He was, however, apprehended. In this era, colonial judges in Australia often handed out extremely harsh sentences for even petty crimes in order to secure the manual labour required to build the roads and support the nation's developing infrastructure.

Mad Dog Morgan came at a time when the Australian film industry was beginning to gain critical recognition. What followed in subsequent years was an explosion of the so-called Ozploitation films, a genre of bloody, violent, and often dystopian movies such as *Mad Max* (1979) and *Turkey Shoot* (1982). These films show the bleak landscape of the Australian outback and revel in extreme violence. Just as Hopper was present at the beginning of the New Hollywood era, he was also an advocate of the emerging Australian film market, a system that has stayed brazenly independent and controversial since its inception. *Mad Dog Morgan* remains a vicious film, not dulled in any way by the thirty-five years since it was made. It remains brave and honest in its depiction of not only the workers who built the modern Australia but of the Aboriginal peoples and the harsh and often criminal abuse bestowed upon them by their colonists. *Mad Dog Morgan* is a testament to Hopper's creativity and his refusal, at least at this point in his career, to accept compromise.

An example of Dennis Hopper's era-defining work was in writer and director Henry Jaglom's film *Tracks* (1977), a post-Vietnam war movie which like *Apocalypse Now* dealt with the madness of war but from a much more internalised and surrealist perspective. As described by Jamie Russell, "*Tracks* takes the disorientated states of altered consciousness as its aesthetic starting point."[20] It is literally a film in which reality and the subconscious blur. Hopper portrays young Sergeant Jack Falen, returning home from serving in Vietnam with the body of his dead service buddy in tow. He travels across country by train, a journey that takes several days. Sergeant Falen is a troubled and awkward individual who seems unable to adapt to life outside of the war. He stumbles from coach to coach dropping in on his fellow passengers' conversations, hallucinating gruesome acts of sexual violence, and becoming increasingly paranoid as the journey continues towards its destination. When he arrives, we assume, in his hometown, he pays a visit to places that seem familiar and comforting to him. However, psychologically, Sergeant Falen is no longer the man he was when he left the town to fight the war. His instability becomes even more apparent at the funeral of his friend. Expecting a ticker tape parade, the funeral is only attended by three army officials and the minister. Upset that his friend has been so disregarded, he asks for some time alone to reflect and say goodbye. When the uncaring senior officers leave him alone, Sergeant Falen begins a seething monologue of hatred aimed straight at the people and the country that sent him to war. The urgency of his repeated words reveals the full fear and desperation of post-traumatic stress disorder. Originally a scripted monologue that ran many pages long and called into question the war, Hopper chose instead to improvise a conflicted and inarticulate speech full of rage that becomes a more honest reflection of Sergeant Falen's feelings towards his country. At this point, Sergeant Falen jumps into the hole in front of him, opens the casket and unveils not the dead body of his friend, but an arsenal of weapons and ammunition. He suits up and brings the trauma of war to the very doorsteps of those individuals whom repeatedly inform him how they wish they had been there on the front lines with him.

Not long after filming had finally wrapped on the epic *Apocalypse Now* in 1977, Hopper cleaned up his physical appearance and headed over to Germany to appear as career criminal and art forger Tom Ripley in German director Wim Wenders' *The American Friend* (1977), an adaptation of Patricia Highsmith's popular 1974 novel *Ripley's Game*. Hopper's turn in *The American Friend* offers a performance of beautiful subtlety and underlying menace and is certainly different from the suave literary character, as David Tacon remarks in an article for *Senses of Cinema*:

> Dennis Hopper cuts a, at times, bizarre figure as the sinister Tom Ripley, a loner, a cowboy adrift in Hamburg, consumed with existential anguish over his betrayal of Jonathan Zimmermann, a terminally ill picture framer, whom Ripley has coerced into becoming an assassin. Hopper's characterization must have been a shock to Highsmith purists, but highly enjoyable for the rest of us.[21]

Both the late 1970s and the early 1980s saw Hopper embrace European art cinema more than he ever had or ever would again. 1978's *Couleur Chair* (*Flesh Colour*) saw Hopper play a photographer called Mel, and in the Spanish film *Las Flores del Vicio* (*Bloodbath*, 1979), Hopper is a drug-addicted poet named Chicken. In the 1984 Swedish film *Slagskämpen* (*The Inside Man*), Hopper plays a US government official during the Cold War. Hopper only appeared in a handful of films on American soil during this time. Europe, however, embraced Dennis Hopper with open arms, and this perhaps explains why in European art and film circles, Hopper has been recognised and honoured more as an artist/filmmaker than in his own country, as evidenced by his continuing retrospectives, and his receiving the title of Commander in France's National Order of Arts and Letters in 2008.

Director Francis Ford Coppola steered the ship of crazies that would produce one of the most provocative films in cinematic history: *Apocalypse Now*. Hopper's role was small but pivotal to the film. Based loosely on Joseph Conrad's early-twentieth-century novel *Heart of Darkness*, Coppola transferred the setting from the colonial Congo of the late nineteenth century to war-ravaged Vietnam of the late 1960s. Martin Sheen's already war-damaged military officer, Captain Benjamin Willard, grows increasingly disillusioned with the world and the war as he journeys the Nung River to track down and execute the distinguished and decorated Colonel Kurtz (played by Marlon Brando), an officer who has now gone insane deep in the Cambodian jungle. Martin Sheen's philosophical monologues drive the film towards a standoff outside of Kurtz's empirical compound and Hopper's hyperactive photojournalist makes his entrance with the line: "I'm an American!"

What Hopper achieves with the minor character of the photojournalist is dazzling. He burns the screen with his rapid-fire, thousand-thoughts-a-second ranting and raving, his hand movements forcing the audience to comprehend every syllable of pseudo-philosophical rambling that, as historian and film critic, Jean-Baptiste Thoret comments "make his lines sound like a stuck record".[22] Hopper adds an injection of insanity that invigorates the film. He distils the madness of war and represents the archetype of a person suffering from post-traumatic stress brought on by the horror of conflict. Although the photojournalist has escaped from the external ravages of frontline reportage by subsuming himself into the depths of Kurtz's world, there is no true escape. The war is now internal. Having been transformed by Kurtz's power, Hopper's photojournalist cannot distinguish the wrongdoings of the compound. His rants of "I'm a little man, I'm a little man, he's, he's a great man... I should have been a pair of ragged claws scuttling across the floors of silent seas" clearly demonstrates the state of his shattered mind, his devotion to his master (Kurtz), and also the futility of his own position within the compound (that of the jester). Hopper's portrayal of a war-torn journalist brings to mind Pulitzer-nominated war journalist Chris Hedges' description of his own fall into post-traumatic stress during his reportage in Central America: "By the end I had a nervous twitch in my face...war's sickness had become mine."[23] Although Hedges' external war was a different one, the internal conflict was the same. Hopper's performance elevates the film's narrative with an injection of real madness. He is not alone in doing this. *Apocalypse Now* is a film where the viewer is waiting for sparks to alleviate the brooding narrative. The film is littered with cameo appearances: a solemn captain played by a young and barely recognisable Harrison Ford, Robert Duvall as the unscathed Colonel Kilgore, and the ever-sprightly Playboy Bunnies. It is a film of long stretches, punctuated by riveting moments that make it well worth the long haul.

It is crucial to remember that from the filming of *Easy Rider's* directorial follow up, *The Last Movie* and onwards, Hopper was a drug addict and alcoholic. In Hopper's own words he was "...an alcoholic. People would ask me what drugs I used, and I'd say, "Oh a little coke, some marijuana, but I'm really taking drugs to hide the fact that I'm an alcoholic."[24] The wild-eyed creature that violates *Apocalypse Now* with his frenzied preaching appears to mirror Hopper's state of mind at that time: a drug-fuelled extremist, too far gone, and only capable of playing on-screen crazies to compliment his off-screen persona. This is particularly apparent in Eleanor Coppola's documentary film, *Hearts of Darkness: A Filmmaker's Apocalypse* (1991), as Hopper and Francis Ford Coppola banter back and forth over dialogue. There seems to be no line drawn between character and actor, as Hopper dispenses nonsense in much the same style as the photojournalist. Although his drug and alcohol addictions lasted well into the mid-1980s, it is fascinating to realise that a character such as *Blue Velvet's* Frank Booth, who was far more unstable and violently insane than the photojournalist, or Sergeant Jack Falen, was played by a clean and sober Hopper. *Blue Velvet* came at a time when Hopper was attempting to reinvent himself as an artist and actor and seeking to leave his substance abuse and the wild times behind.

The Return to Hollywood

After a number of years in the wilderness, Hopper was still ostracised by Hollywood's movie moguls and film directors who were simply too frightened to work with his unpredictability. During the early 1980s, Hopper was relegated to minor if still adequate roles in Francis Ford Coppola's youth film *Rumble Fish* (1983) and Sam Peckinpah's crime thriller *The Osterman Weekend* (1983). He also appeared in oddities such as *King of the Mountain* (1981) and *Neil Young: Human Highway* (1982). Hopper began to regain ground in what was a very different Hollywood system to the one he had revolutionised over a decade ago. Gone from the mainstream were the personal auteur movies of the early 1970s; instead there were big budget blockbusters and shallow teen comedies that defined the Ronald Reagan era of unimaginable wealth and patriotism. Simultaneously, there was a blossoming independent scene that kept the more adventurous cinema audience satisfied, but this remained mostly under the radar of popular cinema.

In 1980, Dennis Hopper was cast as the abusive father Don Barnes in a small Canadian television film, at the time entitled *The Case of Cindy Barnes*. The inexperienced director Leonard Yakir soon jumped ship after two weeks of shooting turned up no usable footage. The project was all but abandoned by the cast and crew. Seeing an opportunity to direct the project, Hopper convinced the producers of the film to give him a shot. The producers agreed, as long as Hopper could complete the film on time and within budget. Taking control of the production, Hopper rewrote the melodramatic script and cast the film in a much darker and nihilistic light. He reduced a number of key characters to small roles, shot the film in four weeks, and completed editing in two weeks. The finished film, *Out of the Blue*, was one of the most uncompromising and disturbing films of the early 1980s. Predictably, it was a commercial failure. However, this failure came from the provocative subject matter of child abuse, incest, and the corrosion of the American family unit, hardly a positive selling point to an American audience wishing to embrace a more positive and conservative outlook of family values and patriotic vigour that was being endorsed by the administration of Ronald Reagan. *Out of the Blue* was better received critically and commercially in the European market, although it remained banned in the UK until 1987. The film gathered a cult following, with audiences seeking it out at late-night theatre screenings and pirated videocassette copies. Hollywood did not come crawling back apologetically, as Hopper had hoped it would. Hopper had succeeded in producing a film that was so disconnected from the mood in America that nobody in their right minds would dare to let him direct again.

Francis Ford Coppola's 1984 gang film *Rumble Fish* was something of a double bill with his 1983 adaptation of *The Outsiders*. Both these films were adapted from S. E. Hinton's seminal teenage gang novels that also dealt with the subject of gang violence and teenage disillusion. The two films also shared a pack of young and talented actors, with *Rumble Fish* boasting youthful performances from Matt Dillon, Mickey Rourke, Chris Penn, and Nicolas Cage, and *The Outsiders* bearing witness to a pre-superstar Tom Cruise and Patrick Swayze. The Father, as Hopper's character is known, is ravaged by booze and projects a careless quality and a desire to hide away from the world behind a blanket of whiskey. This role, like the photojournalist in *Apocalypse Now*, is again an example of Hopper's unpredictable nature transferred to the screen, as Hopper himself was, at the time of filming, still under the influence of his addictions and presented, in Chris Hoddenfield's powerful description, "the face of a human train wreck".[25] Hopper plays the role with a layer of sweat leaking from underneath his tattered suit, as if his very soul is oozing out of his skin. Although only a minor role, Hopper ensures that his presence is felt, delivering what dialogue he has with thought and precision. One scene in particular stands out from the whole. Rusty James (Matt Dillion) and the Motorcycle Boy (Mickey Rourke) find their father swigging a drink by himself in a local bar. When he sees his two sons enter the bar, Hopper performs a frustrated clench of the teeth and hands, aware that his peace is about to be broken. When his two sons take a seat, the father character explains to Rusty James the conflict of emotions his brother is facing:

> Every now and then, a person comes along, has a different view of the world than does the usual person. It doesn't make them crazy. I mean... an acute perception, man...that doesn't, that doesn't make you crazy.

Rusty James—too young or too dumb to comprehend this concept—is then given a more simplistic explanation:

> He's merely miscast in the play. He was born in the wrong era, on the wrong side of the river...with the ability to be able to do anything that he wants to do and finding' nothing' that he wants to do. I mean nothing.

Although taken from the source novel, the dialogue could have been written specifically for Hopper to perform. In the context of Hopper's circumstances at this point—a collision of past success, present personal failure, and future accomplishments in film and art—it proves a deeply symbolic, prophetic statement.

In 1986, Hopper nailed three key performances. Shooter, the alcoholic ex-basketball coach trying to make peace with his estranged son in the sports film *Hoosiers* bagged him an Oscar nomination for Best Supporting Actor. The troubled ex-biker Feck in Tim Hunter's gloomy teen drama *River's Edge* was a stunning performance of quiet and complex guilt, with a subtle touch of eccentric humour. However, it was Hopper's triumph of twisted anger and childish brutality in *Blue Velvet* that really proved that Hopper was back on form. Set in the small, seemingly idyllic town of Lumberton, Hopper's sudden appearance as the psychotic local crook Frank Booth reveals a dark underbelly of sinister proportions.

The director of *Blue Velvet*, David Lynch, had just gone through the disastrous experience of filming the big-budget movie *Dune* (1984) and was now ready to take a purposeful step towards a smaller budget and creative control. With *Blue Velvet*, Lynch produced the stand-out film of 1980s independent cinema. The early 1980s was full of films that portrayed teenagers as over-privileged rich kids whose lust for danger never had any lasting consequence. Even the supposedly rebellious kids in iconic 1980s films, such as the teen comedies directed by John Hughes—*Sixteen Candles* (1984) and *Breakfast Club* (1985)—came from relatively middle-class happy homes and are eventually redeemed in the eyes of their peers and elders. *Blue Velvet* changed that ideal. Kyle MacLachlan's character, the naive Jeffrey Beaumont, would ultimately pay the emotional price for all those supposed delinquents of the 1980s era. Jeffrey's transition from boy to man at the hands of Frank Booth is a devastating journey of lost innocence. Suddenly, young people had to answer for their curiosity, and the effects were severe and long term.

The arrival of Frank Booth changes everything, including the momentum of the narrative itself. At one point, as Frank loudly proclaims, "Let's fuck! I'll fuck anything that moves!", Frank and his cronies disappear from the screen, leaving the camera to linger on an empty room for a matter of seconds; the urgency that Frank brings is too fast even for the frame rate to keep up. To refer back to Nicholas Rombes' analysis of *Blue Velvet*, what appears to happen here is "...a radical cut, that will *alter the balance of power*, that will shift the *Blue Velvet* into magic realism for a split second, throwing into turmoil the realism of the film."[26] The point at which Frank disappears from the screen is certainly unnerving. The viewer is left to imagine that Frank must have otherworldly power or be a conjuror of some black magic. Certainly the lives of those around Frank are twisted to serve his perverse sexual and violent urges or his dubious criminal dealings. For such a vile creature, he is able to cast a wide spell over many, including Jeffery. At the moment Frank races ahead of the film, the audience follows him into a murky underworld where the characters are robbed of their innocence, where foul language reaches astronomical proportions, where Dean Stockwell as the suave freak Ben lip-synchs Roy Orbison's mournful 'In Dreams'. The film revels in its psychosis, transforming it from a hokey teen investigation into a twisted cat-and-mouse game and serves as a biting commentary on the darkness that exists beneath the gloss of the American Dream.

In *River's Edge*, Hopper's character, the local weirdo Feck, makes a living dealing out joints of weed to the neighbourhood teenagers and loves divulging tales of his youthful exploits as a member of a motorcycle gang, confessing with much enthusiasm "I ate so much pussy in those days; my beard looked like a glazed doughnut." Feck also divulges to the teens that he is a fugitive from the law for a crime of passion: "I killed a girl, it was no accident. Put a gun to the back of her head and blew her brains right out the front. I was in love." Thus to avoid capture, Feck remains a recluse, never venturing outside of his house. The only company he keeps is a blow-up sex doll called Elly. The teenagers who populate the small town are an aimless gang of misfits. Smoking grass and drinking beer appear to be the only vices that satisfy them. When one of their friends, John, strangles his girlfriend by the banks of a river, the gang takes action to try to protect him.

Hopper's scenes are tinged with an eccentric humour, such as when Feck slow dances with his blow-up sex doll, or his many interactions with the jittery amphetamine-enthusiast Lane (Crispin Glover). Hopper's most notable and emotional scene is when Feck is hiding out with the young murderer, John, by the banks of the river. Asked by the gloating John what it felt like when he pulled the trigger on the girl he loved, Feck responds, "It was something I did. I don't know if you can understand, I loved her." Tears well up in Feck's eyes as John explains how powerful he felt at the moment he strangled her, but now he just feels lost and alone. Feck sweetly offers, "I'll be your friend."

Throughout most of the film, the emotions of the gang of teenagers are repressed under a veneer of cold detachment. Feck's tear-jerking confessional about the girl he killed when he was a young man is filled with sadness, yet he shows no regret for his actions, he believes what he did was the right thing to do, the correct way to express his love. In the end, he reacts the same way he did in the past by shooting John in the head to end his torment and thus showing how much he cares for him. In a film that confronts the numbness of feelings from its young cast, Hopper acts as the emotional catharsis of the film.

Hopper received an academy-award nomination for Best Supporting Actor for his role as Wilbur 'Shooter' Flatch in *Hoosiers,* a basketball film set in the mid-1950s with a lead performance from Gene Hackman as Coach Norman Dale. Shooter, a once-promising basketball coach, is now the town drunk and the estranged father to one of the basketball team's star players. Shooter is a man of mixed-up emotions and long-lost hope. He is labelled as troublesome by the residents of town and by his own son. He lives as an outcast in a cabin in the woodlands that lies on the edge of town. He spends his days drowning his sorrows in whiskey. Although not dissimilar to his role as the drunkard father in *Rumble Fish*, Hopper bestows on Shooter a deeper range of emotions and gives him a shot at redemption that Hopper's past characters never really get. Coach Dale asks Shooter to become his deputy coach, providing he cleans himself up and quits drinking. At first nervous that he will fall off the proverbial wagon, Shooter eventually gains confidence in coaching the team. Shooter admits to Coach Dale: "I know everything there is to know about the greatest game ever invented." For a time, Shooter does bring to the team a cohesion and a winning streak. However, feeling the pressure when the team makes it to the finals, he returns to the bottle once again, making a public nuisance of himself and embarrassing his son at the team's penultimate game. This being his last chance, Shooter is sent to hospital to recover from his alcohol addiction. He listens to the team's championship game on the radio from his hospital bed. Out of the three key performances of 1986, it is clear why Hopper was praised for his role in *Hoosiers*. Compared to the depravity of Frank Booth and the eccentricities of Feck, the character of Shooter is about as uplifting as Hopper could get. Although not as fast-paced or as emotive as some modern sports movies, *Hoosiers* has earned a much-deserved reputation as one of the greatest and most authentic sports films.

After such an astounding comeback, Hopper renewed his directorial ambitions in what seemed an unlikely source material but could be seen as a continuation of Hopper's post-1960s documentation. Writer and poet Charles Bukowski had produced an autobiographical screenplay called *Barfly*, which had been commissioned by French film director Bardot Schroeder. Bukowski was keen to see Sean Penn in the lead role as Henry Chinaski, Bukowski's literary alter-ego. Penn was interested in the project on the condition that Hopper direct the film. However, Bukowski's distrust of Hopper and his loyalty to Schroeder led to the project falling through. Schroeder went on to direct the film with Mickey Rourke in the lead role.

Sean Penn wanted to find a project for himself and Hopper to work on together, and in his search he came across an interesting screenplay. The original script was set in Chicago and revolved around a gang who had invented a new type of addictive drug based on cough syrup. When Hopper met with Orion, the film's producer "he told them it was awful, terrible - that it wouldn't even make a bad television show."[27] Much like the narrative overhaul he gave *Out of the Blue*, Hopper changed the location of *Colors* to Los Angeles and placed the action right in the nerve centre of the longstanding gang warfare between The Crips and The Bloods. The film follows young hot-headed rookie police officer Danny McGavin (Sean Penn) and the seasoned and mature officer Bob Hodges (Robert Duvall) as they attempt to alleviate the tensions between the gangs. The film was a massive critical and commercial success. It also boasted a soundtrack of hip-hop standards that promoted the genre to a wider audience. Hopper's invigorated direction offers a kinetic charge and allows the action and locations to become immersive. As Janet Maslin's review in *The New York Times* points out: "The look of this film, with its hard-edged, brightly sunlit urban settings and its constant threat of unanticipated motion, is genuinely three-dimensional and utterly enveloping."[28] After the generational summarising of *Easy Rider*, the experimental mosaic of *The Last Movie*, and the nihilistic sickening of *Out of the Blue*, with *Colors* Hopper achieves a genuine balance of powerful cultural critiquing fused with commercial cinematic entertainment.

The Action Man of 1990s Cinema

Dennis Hopper's post-*Blue Velvet* career is littered with Frank Booth stereotypes. Tobe Hooper's horror rehash *Texas Chainsaw Massacre 2* (1986) saw Hopper wield a chainsaw in manic fashion, shouting at the top of his lungs and preaching vengeance. John Dahl's noir thriller *Red Rock West* (1993) saw Hopper in the role of Lyle, a menacing hitman with a sneering Southern twang. *Blue Velvet* alerted mainstream Hollywood that they now had a go-to actor for the standard bad guy. Thus, audiences were treated to watered-down and comical versions of Frank Booth, including Hopper sporting a fetching codpiece and eye patch as the bad guy Deacon in Kevin Reynolds' massively expensive *Waterworld* (1995). His take on reptilian dictator King Koopa in *Super Mario Bros* (1993), Rocky Morton and Annabel Jankel's adaptation of the eponymous video game, was farcical. In Jan De Bont's high-octane action movie *Speed* (1994), Hopper plays retired bomb disposal expert turned bomb terrorist Howard Payne, perfecting the art of laughing manically whilst delivering snide one-liners ("pop quiz hotshot"). To say that Hopper was stereotyped as a Frank Booth madman is to understate Hopper's ability. But the ghost of Frank Booth haunted the remainder of Hopper's career and even his own off-screen persona. The role had such a huge impact within popular culture that it is incredibly difficult to separate Frank Booth from Dennis Hopper and his subsequent roles. That being said, the 1990s also provided Hopper with ample opportunity to direct films. His first three directorial films had been spread out over three decades and had been mired with egotism, drug abuse, iconoclast aspirations, and the temptations of fame. In the 1990s, Hopper directed three films in fairly quick succession. Was this a case of making up for lost time on Hopper's part?

Hopper started the decade as a director. His fifth film, *Catchfire*, was a thriller about a hitman who falls in love with his prey. It was Hopper's attempt to "make a classic film with a beginning, a middle and an end. A linear film that everyone can enjoy."[29] *Catchfire* was released under the directorial pseudonym Alan Smithee, a name used by directors to publically disown a film when producers or television executives re-edit their work out of its original intention. The film's distributor Vestron pictures took Hopper's 180-minute cut and hacked it down to 98 minutes. Two years later, Hopper eventually re-edited *Catchfire* and re-released it under the title *Backtrack* under his own name. With production and editing removed from his control, the film was reduced to being an uneven mesh of gangster genre, road movie, and romance, despite an intriguing premise of a conceptual artist, played by Jodie Foster, channelling real conceptual artist Jenny Holzer, who witnesses a mob hit and has to go into hiding. The man contracted to track her down—Milo, played by Hopper—falls in love with her, and the two become unlikely companions. Hopper's direction attempts to mix his love of modern art with a genre thriller. The film features some impressive art installations from Jenny Holzer's *Truism* works (1977-9) that includes lines of scrolling digitized text proclaiming, "KILLING IS UNAVOIDABLE BUT IS NOTHING TO BE PROUD OF" and "PROTECT ME FROM WHAT I WANT". The film also features an appearance by Bob Dylan creating a relief sculpture.

During the 1960s, Hopper was an avid photographer. One of his most famous photographs is titled *Double Standard*. It depicts the black-and-white view from a car's front window frame, its dashboard and rear view mirror framing the scene outside the car. The landscape directly ahead is that of the two roads which lay at the intersection of Melrose Avenue, North Doheny Drive, and Santa Monica Boulevard veering off to each side of the picture. It looks like a typical mid-American town of the early 1960s. Hopper's sixth directorial effort, *The Hot Spot* (1990), looks as if it takes place within a now-colourised frame of *Double Standard*. The film is set within a "contemporary Texas town so sleepy and backward, it seems to have stopped evolving sometime around Eisenhower."[30] The low-rise buildings, the wide and deserted avenues, and the used car lots dominate the film's locations. The story concerns handsome drifter Harry Madox (Don Johnson), who takes a job as a car salesman and becomes embroiled in a sexual affair with his boss George Hershaw's wife Dolly (Virginia Madsen). He also develops an interest in the car dealership's secretary Gloria (Jennifer Connelly), who is being bribed by a local man, Frank Sutton, who has nude photographs of her and one of her girlfriend's fooling around.

Dennis Hopper's handling of *The Hot Spot* feels like the slow turning of pages of a pulp noir paperback. In fact, *The Hot Spot* was an adaptation of Charles Williams' hardboiled 1953 novel *Hell Hath No Fury,* originally adapted in 1962 and intended for Robert Mitchum. The screenplay was updated by Hopper to a more contemporary setting, though the film feels soaked in the past. Hopper's direction is deliberately slow and "borrows its languid rhythms from a scorching sun that slows life down to a crawl and coats the cast with an ever-present layer of perspiration".[31] The consistent free-flowing rhythms of the jazz and blues soundtrack (discussed in the essay 'Hip-Hopp: Dennis Hopper and Music') give the film an impression of overbearing heat and queasiness. It is also Hopper's most measured film. No culture-defining aspects are present as such, though there is a sense of artistic intent with the *Coca-Cola* sign appearing on numerous occasions in a reference to its use in pop art by artist Andy Warhol.

In 1993, the screenplay for *True Romance,* directed by Tony Scott, signalled a vibrant new voice in modern cinema. Quentin Tarrantino had been writing screenplays for a number of years and had directed his first independent feature *Reservoir Dogs* (1992) to much acclaim. His subsequent movies would define the next decade in independent cinema. His kinetic style of filmmaking, snappy dialogue, and pop culture references would often be replicated throughout the decade. Hopper's role as Clifford Worley, the ex-cop and recovering-alcoholic father to Christian Slater's erratic and irresponsible Clarence resembles past roles in which Hopper is the troubled father figure. Clifford is, however, different from those past characters: for one, he carries a dignity that Hopper's past father figures never attain. The interrogation scene Hopper shares with Christopher Walken as mobster Vincenzo Coccotti is all at once menacing, funny, and heartbreaking. Clarence and his new wife (and ex-prostitute) Alabama, played by Patricia Arquette, pay a visit to Clifford. Clarence tells his father that he has killed Alabama's vicious pimp Drexl Spivey (Gary Oldman), and wants to know if he is in the frame. Clifford contacts his old colleagues on the force on behalf of his son, and no leads are found. Clarence and Alabama leave for Los Angeles with a suitcase of Drexl's drugs they hope to sell in Los Angeles. However, Drexl's bosses uncover Clarence's driver's licence that leads them directly to Clifford. Clifford is roughed up by a group of thugs who seat him face-to-face with Vincenzo Coccotti. Coming to the realisation that he is going to die for his son's stupidity, he accepts his fate and plays Coccotti at his own game. The scene offers a relative calm amidst the storm of Tony Scott's high-octane film of snappy dialogue, stylistic editing, pop culture references, and an abundance of cameo appearances ranging from Brad Pitt as a lazy stoner, Gary Oldman as Drexl, Samuel L Jackson as a drug dealer, and Val Kilmer as an imaginary Elvis Presley. Hopper's shining moment comes when he calmly delivers a monologue insulting Coccotti's Sicilian ancestry and claiming that the dark skin of Sicilians is directly descended from the Moors. It is a move that saves him from being tortured by Coccotti's thugs. He rounds off his monologue with: "it's absolutely amazing to me to think that to this day, hundreds of years later, that, uh, that Sicilians still carry that nigger gene." Clifford quietly savors his last puff of a cigar before Coccotti ruthlessly puts a bullet in his head. Christopher Walken compared the scene to a dance: "I started out as a dancer, and Hopper and I partner well together."[32] In a film that is at times overly kinetic, the scene between Hopper and Walken is a slow dance amongst the chaos.

The narrative of two delinquents on the run, engaging in a mindless crime spree, was something of a staple of 1990s cinema that harked back to the popularity of the 1960s and 1970s road movie—films such as Terrence Malick's *Badlands* (1973), Arthur Penn's *Bonnie and Clyde* (1967), and to a lesser degree, *Easy Rider.* The 1990s equivalents, such as Ridley Scott's *Thelma and Louise* (1991), Oliver Stone's *Natural Born Killers* (1994), and Dominic Sena's *Kalifornia* (1993), all relied heavily on the pop culture referencing and iconography of the road movie that *Easy Rider* and its genre defined. *True Romance* shares these principal elements with the above-mentioned movies. It seems fitting that Dennis Hopper carried the baton of the road movie genre from one era to another.

Neo-noir thriller *Red Rock West* offers a Frank Booth hit without having to delve into the murky underworld of David Lynch's warped mind. Dennis Hopper's role as hired hitman Lyle from Dallas plays up to the bad guy stereotype that Hopper was cultivating after his performance in *Blue Velvet* and that came to fruition in *Speed, Super Mario Brothers* and *Waterworld. Red Rock West* is the story of Wayne (J.T. Walsh), a backstabbing husband who hires the formidable Lyle to kill his wife Suzanne (Lara Flynn Boyle) in order to claim on her life insurance. By coincidence, Dallas-native Michael (Nicolas Cage) also happens to arrive in town looking for work on an oil crew and, upon wandering into Wayne's bar, is mistaken for Lyle. Desperate for a job, Michael plays along and accepts the hit. That is, until the real Lyle arrives in town and Michael falls for Suzanne. What follows is a cat-and-mouse chase across the dusty plains of Red Rock. Roger Ebert stated in a review that: "Hopper plays a version of the character he has become famous for: the smiling, charming, cold blooded killer with a screw loose."[32] Ebert nails the comparisons with ghosts of characters past. Initially only considered a straight-to-video thriller with not much mainstream potential, the film was screened at the Toronto Film Festival and eventually played in small art house theatres across America. Despite the film's apparent un-marketability, *Red Rock West* is an intelligently dumb movie, a very rare entity that seems to cross an otherwise impenetrable barrier between mainstream acceptance and art house cool.

Hopper's final feature-length directorial film (in 2000, he directed an eight-minute short film entitled *Homeless*) was the action comedy *Chasers* (1994). The film paired Tom Berenger and William McNamara as two US Navy shore patrol officers sent to escort a young female prisoner (Erika Eleniak). When Hopper stated in the 1971 interview with Merv Griffin that he would "simplify and romanticise" his work in order to "identify with an audience", *Chasers* must have been the film he had in mind. The film is certainly one of Hopper's most mainstream products, yet as a paradox it remains his least commercially and critically acclaimed film. It lacks many of Hopper's artistic intentions and cultural significances. Even the film's soundtrack—an important feature of a Dennis Hopper film—is unfulfilling. The film's saving grace is the off-kilter cameo performances that litter the narrative: Crispin Glover as a freaked-out and nervy naval officer, Gary Busey as a wild-eyed captain, Dean Stockwell as a car salesman, Hopper himself even appears as a pervy ladies underwear salesman whose nickname is Doggie. A review of the film in *The New York Times* comments that "Hopper can be counted on to fill the sidelines of a film with amusing wild-card diversions, even if he has more trouble holding together a central plot".[33] This is the film's actual triumph. Hopper's divergent tactics takes the audience away from the rather flimsy and cliché-ridden narrative.

For the action blockbuster genre that it operates within, *Speed* is actually a minuscule film that was made on a twenty-eight-million-dollar budget by Dutch cinematographer Jan De Bont (*Die Hard, Basic Instinct*) in his debut as director. The film launched the career of Sandra Bullock and steered Keanu Reeves from his earlier roles as airhead stoners (*Bill and Ted's Excellent Adventure*) to men of action (*The Matrix*). What is most significant about *Speed's* extraordinary success is what it allowed subsequent action films to achieve. Action films of the 1980s tended towards a fantastical, unreal quality. Films such as Ridley Scott's *Alien* (1979) and its sequel *Aliens* (1986), James Cameron's *Terminator* (1984), and John McTiernan's *Predator* (1987) all contained something otherworldly, grotesque aliens, or indestructible future cyborgs—not substantial or real enough to elicit concrete fear or anxiety from everyday circumstances. The 1990s was the decade of a more realistic, grittier action film steeped in the mundane, revelling in the anxieties of ordinary people. The advent of *Speed* has led to what some audiences might deem as guilty pleasures, such as *Con Air* (1997), in which prison inmates hijack a plane, and *Face/Off* (1997), in which Nicolas Cage and John Travolta hijack each other's faces. These films share a common thread, being of stock summer blockbuster fluff. They are films produced to entertain huge audiences the world over.

Hopper's bomb terrorist Howard Payne is no stretch for his acting style. The character fits with the persona of typical action-movie bad guys that is representative throughout cinema. The seemingly evil intent of world domination or sadistic revenge is neither explained in-depth nor justified. The bad guys are bad, plain and simple, and this requires that the good guys stop them, whatever the cost to the cities they often demolish or the innocents they indiscriminately eliminate in order to achieve that. Hopper, at the time of the film's release, seemed to believe *Speed* pointed towards a reinvention within the genre: "in a sense, I think it is revolutionary... I think when you look back at this period of time you will have to look back at *Speed* and say: That is really what an action movie really should have been—and was."[34] I would propose that Hopper was right: at least for a short period of time, the action genre saw fit to update its criteria to the modern world. Ultimately, *Speed* works because it is executed right, and played as simple popcorn entertainment.

It seems short-sighted to end this summary of Hopper's film work in the mid-1990s. After all, still to come was big-budget epic *Waterworld* (1995), the delirious *Search and Destroy* (1995), the eloquent *Basquait* (1996), the dark and moody *The Blackout* (1997)—films that featured Hopper engaged in artistic creation. However, this period of Hopper's career also begins to feature an array of straight-to-video and dire television movies such as *Space Truckers* (1996), *Tycus* (1998), *Lured Innocence* (1999), and *The Prophets Game* (1999), to name but a few. These movies tested audiences' patience with cheap visual effects and stilted performances. This trend continued into the last decade of Dennis Hopper's career, somewhat tarnishing his well-earned reputation. Films such as *Held for Ransom* (2000), *The Last Ride* (2004), *The Keeper* (2004), *The Crow: Wicked Prayer* (2005), and *House of 9* (2005) featured Hopper amongst mostly unknown actors and putting in a performance which was uncharacteristically monotonous. However, the last decade did include some critically lauded, offbeat roles. Hopper appeared in George Romero's *Land of the Dead* (2005) as Paul Kaufman, a greedy capitalist leader hell-bent on maintaining a corrupt order. Three decades after *The American Friend*, Hopper once again teamed up with Wim Wenders on the film *Palermo Shooting* (2008), playing a Death-like character called Frank who bestows on the film's young protagonist (Campino, singer with German punk band Die Toten Hosen) his theory of photography. His most acclaimed appearance was alongside Sir Ben Kingsley, Patricia Clarkson, and Penélope Cruz as the poet and aging lothario George O'Hearn in the sophisticated drama *Elegy* (2008), director Isobel Coixet's adaptation of Phillip Roth's 2001 novella *The Dying Animal.* Hopper also provided narration to a number of documentaries on varied subjects such as the porn industry in *Inside Deep Throat* (2005), and skateboarding in *Rising Son: The Legend of Skateboarder Christian Hosoi* (2006). Perhaps making clear his importance within popular culture, Hopper also devoted time to being interviewed at length for numerous documentaries such as the New Hollywood exposé *Easy Riders, Raging Bulls: How the Sex-Drugs-and Rock 'N Roll Generation Saved Hollywood* (2003) and talking architecture in *Sketches of Frank Gehry* (2006). His last film appearance in mainstream cinema was voicing a wolf called Tony in the animated film *Alpha and Omega* (2010). He embraced something of a television renaissance, a medium Hopper had not been concerned with since the late 1950s and early 1960s. He appeared in numerous episodes as Russian war criminal Victor Drazen in the immensely popular series *24* (2001-2010). A bizarre and rarely documented excursion to China saw Hopper as the main character Smith in a series called *Flatland* (2002). He then teamed up with Benjamin Bratt in *E-Ring* (2005-2006), a Pentagon-based drama in which Hopper played Colonel Eli McNulty. And finally, he played maniacal record producer Ben Cenders in the series *Crash* (2008-2009), a spin-off from the 2004 film of the same name directed by Paul Haggis about race and class relations in Los Angeles.

Dennis Hopper defined the post-war American century by embodying the essence of each decade and weaving a thread throughout his career of the collapsing American Dream. The young and impressionable 1950s teenager turned on by drugs, rock 'n' roll music, and sex leads to the buoyant hippie of the 1960s embracing the utopian dream of free love, peace, and understanding but ultimately realises the ideal is unobtainable. This disillusion leads to the bewildered and damaged relic of the 1970s, engaged in useless and unwinnable conflicts. When it is truly understood that such conflicts are unwinnable, this leads to a self-serving sociopath and an indulgent quest for power over people, and then finally to the maniac, hell-bent on destruction for what life did not give him. Alongside the cultural significance and era-defining contexts of *Rebel Without a Cause, Easy Rider, Apocalypse Now, Blue Velvet,* and *Speed* are an array of other deeply significant movies that further explore Hopper's cultural concurrences and contradictions. The films I described above form an iconic story of each era and a narrative that forms a historical perspective of post-war America. These films provide cultural reference points for not only Dennis Hopper's film career but also the social and political climates the films were produced in.

Hip-Hopp

Dennis Hopper and Music

Dennis Hopper's relationship with and knowledge of contemporary music greatly influenced his career as a film director. It is important to consider this aspect in order to understand his importance and influence in film and popular culture. Hopper's use of music within his own directorial films placed within them cultural markers that offered commentary on the fictional narratives of the film and the factual events that surround the era in which the film was made. When Hopper incorporated 1960s rock and folk songs into the soundtrack of *Easy Rider's* jaunt across America, they not only provided an entertaining visual and aural experience, they also presented additional significance to the narrative—though in some respects the significance was accidental, as Hopper admitted: "It took me a year to edit it. I would play the radio on the way to the editing room and I would hear the music off the radio. And as I was doing the travelling sequences I started putting songs to it."[1] Originally, the soundtrack was to be scored by folk-rock superstars Crosby, Stills & Nash. However, according to Hopper, the band's ethos didn't correspond with his own and that of his film:

> The original idea was for Crosby, Stills & Nash to score *Easy Rider*, but I had a falling out with Stephen Stills. We were driving back to my office in his limo and I said, "Stephen, this simply isn't going to work." He asked why and I shouted, "Because I've never been in a limo before and anyone who drives around town in a limo can't understand my movie! Fuck off!"[2]

This dramatic disagreement led *Easy Rider* to become a milestone in film sound-tracking. Before *Easy Rider,* it was virtually unheard of for a movie to use already recorded and released music by popular bands and singers on a soundtrack. Prior to *Easy Rider,* the norm for a film soundtrack was for it to be scored by composers or session musicians after an initial edit of the movie was available. As the 1960s progressed, a number of films featured original folk rock scores recorded predominantly by one artist. In the case of *The Graduate* (1967), folk duo Simon & Garfunkel provided original compositions that made up the bulk of the soundtrack material. Alongside the other social, cultural, and otherwise temporary film industry changes *Easy Rider* helped shape, it also laid the foundations for filmmakers to begin to use pre-existing music to soundtrack their films. All that was required was for the producers to pay a fee, or in the context the 1960s, be associates with enough willing musicians. Along with other music-orientated films such as The Beatles' *Help!* (1965) and The Monkees' psychedelic film *Head* (1968), *Easy Rider* acted as a prelude to the creation of music videos that would go on to help create music channels such as MTV and VH1 in the mid-1980s. It is certainly easy to spot the embryonic music video style in these late 1960s movies. The stable of most music videos, such as a quick-fire editing style and use of symbolism to tell a short narrative, can be found throughout *Easy Rider*. According to Andrew Goodwin in his book *Dancing in the Distraction Factory*, this process of film soundtracks leading to music videos was a natural evolution: "in its earliest days rock and roll was promoted via film; indeed many teens first discovered rock at the movies."[3] Now music incorporates film language to promote a song. The musical interludes of *Easy Rider* provide a mosaic of artistic imagery to complement the song and underline its meaning within the film. As we shall see, Dennis Hopper had a tendency to emphasise the narratives using lyrical accompaniment. For example, the imagery for The Byrds' psychedelic standard 'I Wasn't Born to Follow' shows Billy and Wyatt gliding through a rugged sunlit forest, a deep valley running into the far distance, an overshadowing mountain lingering over the landscape, with the sunlight creating prisms of lens flare that absorb the frame. This setting is mirrored in the song' lyrics:

> Journey where the diamond crescent's glowing / and run across the valley / beneath the sacred mountain / and wander through the forest / where the trees have leaves of prisms / and break the light in colors / that no one knows the name of.[4]

For further emphasis, Billy and Wyatt then pull up to a gas station called The Sacred Mountain. The imagery of the film corresponds and complements the lyrical content and vice-versa.

When Hopper followed up *Easy Rider* with *The Last Movie* in 1971, he approached the soundtrack, if not the film itself, in a more traditional way. Hopper recruited singer songwriter Kris Kristofferson to record some original compositions and to add some of his own already released and popular songs to the soundtrack. The key track in *The Last Movie* is Kristofferson's woeful 'Me and Bobby McGee'. However, tying up the folksy Kristofferson compositions is a mosaic of sound featuring bell chimes, clips of muted conversation, and a strummed and discordant guitar. This is reminiscent of the trip scene in *Easy Rider*, which included a rhythmic thumping machine, bells and whistles from the distant Mardi Gras parade, and clipped improvised dialogue from the actors. In this case, the impressive sound design of a short segment of *Easy Rider* is stretched over the entire running time of *The Last Movie*. If *The Last Movie* fails as a narrative piece, the merging of image and mosaic sound is an artistic accomplishment of audio visual stimulation. As *The Last Movie* deals with the production of a Hollywood film and the devastating affects it has on the indigenous people once the crew and cast have vacated, it seems appropriate that Hopper would wish to make further use/misuse of Hollywood clichés and formulaic filmmaking. However, the film takes great pleasure in tearing these clichés apart and breaking the rules. As an accompanying piece to *The Last Movie*, the soundtrack to the documentary *The American Dreamer* is a collection of rambling folk songs 'inspired by' Hopper and his excursion to Peru to film *The Last Movie*. Songs such as 'Screaming Metaphysical Blues' by singer/songwriter John Buck Wilkin make reference to Hopper's Peruvian adventures in banal lines, such as:

> Here's to Mr. Hopper / who has traded in his chopper / for a gamble in the South American sun / he got some heads from Hollywood / who think things might be pretty good / if they can figure out what thing he's done.[5]

A perfect summing up of what Hopper produced and how Universal Pictures felt when Hopper delivered the finished product.

After the critical mauling of *The Last Movie*, Dennis Hopper's next directorial effort would not be for another ten years. *Out of the Blue* is a terrifying portrayal of Ceebee, a young teenage girl destroyed by abuse and violence at the hands of her father Don, played by Hopper. It seems only fitting that the music Hopper chose to soundtrack the film would perfectly capture the loss of childhood innocence and the darkness that followed. Hopper uses songs that summon up a wide experience of emotions. From Elvis Presley's sweet and chirpy though oddly sinister in this particular film's context 'Teddy Bear' to Neil Young's brooding 'My, My, Hey, Hey (Out of the Blue)'. Young's poignant lyrics about how "It's better to burn out than to fade away"[6] perfectly echo the dramatic and nihilistic end of the film where CeeBee, after murdering her abusive father, kills herself and her mother by blowing up her father's truck with dynamite. Hopper captures the darkness that lies at the heart of Young's song. The nihilism within *Out of the Blue* would be echoed in an act fifteen years later in 1994, when Kurt Cobain, singer, guitarist, and lyricist of Seattle rock band Nirvana shot himself, leaving a suicide note that quoted the above lyrics from 'My, My, Hey, Hey (Out of the Blue)'. The film also incorporates live punk rock performances from

Canadian band The Pointed Sticks. Ceebee wanders into a rock club and sees the band performing live. She is invited by the drummer to bash at the skins as the band rattle through a rendition of their song 'Somebody's Mom'. This is the one act of catharsis within the film. Ceebee is allowed to enjoy the moment, and we as the audience experience an invigorating blast of punk that contrasts with Young's sombre theme song. As discussed previously, Hopper's lyrical emphasis is also in play in *Out of the Blue.* However, this highlighting by Hopper is not always successful. In *Out of the Blue*, it borders on the obvious and trite. The film's heroine Ceebee retaliates against a young girl who accuses her father of killing her little brother in a car crash. As the argument escalates, Ceebee smears a blue ice-cream cone over the young girl's face proclaiming: "I've painted your face blue, it looks better that way, and if you don't shut up and get outta here I'm gonna take you out of the blue and put you into the black". Ceebee then hits a button on her tape player and the first chords of Neil Young's 'My, My, Hey, Hey (Out of the Blue)' are broadcast from the speakers.

The triumph of *Out of the Blue* is the trajectory from 1960s music and the ideals of that era to punk rock and its reaction to those ideals. The countercultural ethos that had originated in the 1960s had morphed into a critical backlash in the late 1970s. Punk, although anti-authoritarian and anti-consumerism, was also anti-hippy. The long hair, flared pants, flowery shirts, and peaceful disposition of the hippies had turned into short spiky hair, tight bondage pants, pins, studs, and an aggressive and abrasive posture. The audience of *Easy Rider*, who had embraced peace and understanding, were now in the firing line of punk rock's nihilism.

After a run of lauded performances in *Blue Velvet, Hoosiers*, and *River's Edge,* Hopper got his next chance to direct in 1988 with the Los Angeles-based gang film *Colors*, possibly Hopper's most commercially and critically successful film after *Easy Rider. Colors* deals with the feuds between the Los Angeles posses The Bloods and The Crips, the Hispanic street gangs, and the Los Angeles police's attempts to mediate the tensions. It is hard to picture a middle-aged Hollywood pro directing a modern, urban, and also very real story. Hopper, who at the time was living in one of the tougher neighbourhoods of Venice, California, pulls it off with gusto, producing a film that is sympathetic, action-packed, and ultimately realistic. *Colors* declines to demonise the gang members, painting them instead as moralistic people intent on survival and the protection of their kin. The soundtrack perfectly captures the emerging rap and hip-hop music scene, with influential hip-hop artists such as MC Shan, Ice T, 7A3, Salt-N-Pepa, Roxanne Shante, and Eric B. & Rakim contributing tracks that reflect the lives of the gang members. As quoted in Goodwin's *Dancing in the Distraction Factory,* rap pioneer Chuck D of Public Enemy describes rap music as "the television of black America", a portal into the "events and environments described by the rapper".[7] The use of sampling gun shots, news feeds, police sirens, and musical hooks from past songs creates a visual image that relates back to television. One of the stand-out tracks of *Colors* is MC Shan's 'A Mind is a Terrible Thing to Waste'. This track illustrates the reality of life in a gang:

> Always watchin your back with your hand on your weapon / You blink for a minute and get brutally beaten / Every time you diss the colors it will keep on repeatin / When you say you knew somebody that was a gang member / You can't say you know him, you can only remember / You have to live life all nervous and worried / But joinin a gang means you want to be buried[8]

MC Shan's lyrical statements reflect the lives and circumstances of the film's gang members from their own perspective—that of becoming a gang member for personal safety and status. It also mirrors the experience of black urban youth in America. Ice T's signature song 'Colors' provides a more social statement and forewarns the police that if they "wanna get rid of the gangs / It's gonna take a lot of work / This is no joke man / this is real."[9] Indeed, the gang warfare within LA is still raging to this day. Two months after its release, the *Colors* soundtrack was certified gold in the United States, bringing rap and hip-hop music to a much wider audience.

Hopper's sixth directorial work, *The Hot Spot,* was his take on a steamy noir thriller. Although the film works to some extent, the soundtrack is perhaps its biggest accomplishment. Produced by famed composer Jack Nitzsche, who composed and selected the soundtracks to *One Flew Over the Cuckoo's Nest* (1975) and *Stand by Me* (1986), the soundtrack features blues and jazz legends Miles Davis, John Lee Hooker, and Taj Mahal performing original compositions. As a standalone record, it's an astonishing artefact and again demonstrates that Hopper was well in tune with his film sound tracking if not his choice of directorial material.

Those working within the music industry have also recognised Dennis Hopper's impact within popular culture, and it is now this aspect to which we turn. Although Hopper never released an album of musical performances (unlike his *Easy Rider* co-star Peter Fonda, who released a single 'November Night' in 1967), he contributed and collaborated with many bands and artists on their albums, singles and live performances. The earliest example is possibly his appearance on The Johnny Cash Show in 1971 in which he lent his reedy southern twang to a rendition of Kris Kristofferson's 'The Pilgrim: Chapter 33', a duet with Cash himself. Incidentally, the lyrical content of the song had been written with Hopper (and to some extent Johnny Cash) in mind and his erratic outbursts on the set of *The Last Movie.* The lyrics perfectly sum up Dennis Hopper's late 1960s/early 1970s persona.

> See him wasted on the sidewalk / in his jacket and his jeans / wearing yesterday's misfortune like a smile / once he had a future / full of money, love, and dreams / which he spent like it was going out of style / He's a poet / he's a picker / he's a prophet / he's a pusher / He's a pilgrim and a preacher / and a problem when he's stoned[10]

The performance with Cash is followed by an astounding, under-the-spotlight reading of Rudyard Kipling's poem *If,* in which two lines—"If you can meet with triumph and disaster and treat those two imposters just the same"[11]—read like a précis of Hopper's artistic career. It is a poem he returned to in *Apocalypse Now.* As the erratic photojournalist he stammers "Did you know that *If* is the middle word in *Life?*" Hopper also appeared on the first track of Bob Dylan's 1976 live bootleg recording *Friends and Other Strangers* performing a manic rendition of *If.* This performance and others show that Hopper could have produced a recording of poetry readings if the urge ever took him.

During the post-punk era of the 1980s British rock band The Smiths provided an intellectual flipside to the slash-and-burn aesthetics of the punk movement. The band's lead singer Morrissey wrote deeply miserablist yet oddly humorous lyrics that reflected the dire social circumstances in Britain at the time. The band's artwork often consisted of film stars and starlets as well as images of the formative years of rock 'n' roll. As a double cover to their 1992 *Best of* collection, The Smiths used Hopper's 1961 photographic portrait of a male and female biker sitting side by side in a roadside cafe. Although in no way a collaboration between Hopper and The Smiths (the band had split in 1987), the photo captures a faded glamour that perfectly reflects the band's music and lyrics. Later in 2000, British Indie band Primal Scream sampled dialogue from *Out of the Blue* for their magnificently if slightly ironically titled single 'Kill All Hippies' (interestingly, a decade earlier, Primal Scream had sampled Peter Fonda's dialogue from the 1967 film *The Wild Angels* in their song 'Loaded'). In addition, and perfectly conjuring up the spirit of *Easy Rider* is the brilliantly named British blues-rock band Dennis Hopper Choppers. Hopper's foremost contribution to music came from an unlikely collaboration with the British animated musical project

Gorillaz, a project concocted by Damon Album, singer with the British band Blur, and Jamie Hewlett, a graphic artist. Hopper narrated a spoken word performance to the track 'Fire Coming out of the Monkey's Head' from the band's 2005 album *Demon Days*. Hopper joined the ranks of other Gorillaz contributors such as De La Soul, Roots Manuva, and Neneh Cherry, and the song's theme of hippy idealism being decimated by corruption could have been lifted from one of Hopper's monologues from *The Trip* or *Apocalypse Now*. Hopper also appeared on stage with the band in 2006 at the Apollo Theater in Harlem to perform the song live. Standing at a podium with lyrics to the song out in front of him, Hopper looked like a scholarly professor delivering one of the most bizarre lectures in academic history.

Hopper also worked in the medium of music videos, most often as a performer within the narrative. It is unfortunate that Hopper never leant his artistic ability to the music video as a director. Since the introduction of MTV in the early 1980s, a promotional video for a single was almost obligatory for any band or artist promoting an album. Over the years, music videos became much more sophisticated and wildly more expensive, and in some cases, better constructed than some modern films. The music video really came into its own in the 1980s and began attracting already established movie directors, starting in the early 1980s with Michael Jackson's 'Thriller', directed by John Landis, and 'Bad', released in 1987 and directed by Martin Scorsese. For the first time, promotional videos had bigger budgets than some movies being produced at the time. On the other side of this was music video directors moving into film such as Spike Jonze, director of *Being John Malkovich* (1999), and Michel Gondry, director of *Human Nature* (2001). Hopper's directorial style of colourful imagery and fast editing as well as his background in expressionist art would have benefited the medium greatly.

In 1998, Dennis Hopper appeared in the hugely expensive music video for rap star Puff Daddy's single 'Victory'. The premise of the music video was a rehash of the film *The Running Man* (1987), which was set within a dystopian society that is controlled by television and empirical game show hosts. The original film (based on Stephen King's source novel of the same name) has Arnold Schwarzenegger playing a wrongly convicted and imprisoned military pilot who is forced to enter into The Running Man, a gruesome game show in which he must face off against a series of foes one-on-one, each one of whom he eliminates with his infamous one-liners. Within the narrative of the video for 'Victory', Puff Daddy takes on the Schwarzenegger role, whilst Hopper portrays Victor Castiglione, President of the New World Order, an evil orchestrator of the game and the criminal world. This slight and heavily clichéd role, in which Hopper delivers such lines as "The last thing I need is a stinking martyr", could be seen as a predecessor of Hopper's character Paul Kaufman in *Land of the Dead*, another tyrant holding the puppet strings of supposed law and order. The eight-minute video holds the title of being the sixth most expensive music promo with a budget of $2,700,000. In contrast, and to highlight the importance of an eight-minute music video compared with a film production, the same year that the 'Victory' video was unveiled saw the release of straight-to-video disaster movie *Tycus* (1998) in which Hopper played a character trying to survive badly computerised comets, which had a budget of only $1,000,000.

The 2006 video for *Smiley Faces* by hip-hop/soul duo Gnarls Barkley featured a documentary prologue to the actual music video which featured Dennis Hopper as fictional music historian Milton Pawley and Dean Stockwell as A&R man Sven Rimwinkle describing the overpowering influence of Gnarls Barkley's music on the past 50 years. The fact that Gnarls Barkley were young men and had just released their eclectic debut album was the in-joke of the video. Using the same green screen technology that put Tom Hanks in historical form in the 1960s in *Forrest Gump* (1994), the video features band members Danger Mouse and Cee-Lo Green superimposed and never ageing onto archival footage from the rich tapestry of music history, taking in the Swing era, the 1950s teenybopper explosion, the 1960s hippie scene, the art rock of the 1970s, and the emergence of 1980s hip-hop. The video received five Grammy awards.

In 2008, Hopper was fleetingly reunited with Johnny Cash. Three years after the country singer's death, a number of recordings had been issued posthumously from leftover recording sessions of the singer's collaboration with record producer Rick Rubin and his record label American Recordings. A music video for the song 'God's Gonna Cut You Down' featured thirty seven actors and musicians filmed in grainy black-and-white close-ups that paused, echoed, and moved with the stomping handclaps of the song. Hopper appears only briefly, standing in front of an art piece (possibly one of his own). The lyrics, sung by Cash's rumbling baritone, proclaims: "He spoke to me in a voice so sweet, I thought I heard the shuffle of angels' feet."[12] At the time the video was made, Hopper was in the early stages of pancreatic cancer.

Hopper's acknowledgement and appreciation of music allowed him to become symbiotic with the ever-changing shift in contemporary tastes. He acted "like a mash-up artist or genre-spanning DJ" before the act was ever mainstream. He "employed pop music in his films to make unexpected, sympathetic connections between generations—charting changes in youth culture".[13] Hopper utilised trends in modern music to support his work on a cultural level. The use of folk, rock, and psychedelic standards in *Easy Rider* allowed the film to transcend its biker flick status and become a much more important cultural and cinematic milestone. *The Last Movie* incorporated brooding folk songs by Kris Kristofferson as a hangover from the 1960s positivity. *The Last Movie* was also a triumph in sound art and audio stimulus. *Out of the Blue* mixed punk rock, early Elvis Presley, and Neil Young's brooding acoustics to create an urgent, sinister, and pessimistic understanding of the early 1980s and the decline of the post-1960s optimism. This theme continued in the soundtrack to *Colors*. Hip-hop had taken the cultural cues, urgency, and DIY aesthetics from punk rock and made it reflect the Black-American experience. If we take these examples of Dennis Hopper's work as his intended vision, we see that Hopper encompasses the protest music of the era. In his role as a social and cultural critic, the music of protest and discontent reflected the images Hopper directed, and reflected the hopes and frustrations of his intended audiences. The soundtrack to a Dennis Hopper film is a crucial element to the overall experience. Hopper knew that with the music incorporated into *Easy Rider,* a soundtrack bursting with 1960s icons such as Bob Dylan, The Byrds, and Jimi Hendrix would add cultural weight to the film. Without the found music, *Easy Rider* may have been another run-of-the-mill biker movie in the AIP tradition, with a slightly jazzy soundtrack as, for example, witnessed in *Hells Angels on Wheels* (1967).

Hopper has never shied away from experimentation in art or film, and his musical soundtrack choices reflect this. Even *Easy Rider*'s more populist moments of Dylan, The Byrds, and Steppenwolf are contrasted with 1960s experimental folk duo The Holy Modal Rounders and psychedelic rock band The Electric Prunes. In *Out of the Blue,* Hopper's use of punk rock gives the film a real urgency that makes it seem a fresh and vital piece of filmmaking. The use of rap and hip-hop music in *Colors* is not only significant to the characters of the film but a cultural reflection of the time in which it was made. The upcoming wave of rap and hip-hop was to signal one of the most important shifts in American music and culture since the 1960s.

The Elephant in the Room

Dennis Hopper and American Politics

An icon of the counterculture and an activist during the social upheaval of the 1960s, Dennis Hopper was, according to himself, "probably as Left as you could get without being a Communist."[1] Nevertheless, in the early 1980s, he switched political allegiances and began supporting the Republican Party. This change came just as the right-wing administration of Ronald Reagan came to power in 1981. Hopper admitted: "I've been a Republican since Reagan. I voted for Bush and his father. I don't tell a lot of people, because I live in a city where somebody who voted for Bush is really an outcast."[2] The city in question was Los Angeles, California, a state that George W. Bush lost to Democratic nominee Al Gore in the 2000 election (although his father, George Bush Senior, enjoyed a better result in the 1988 election campaign). Reagan's administration signified a radical shift in internal and external policies. As outlined in Leonard Quart and Albert Auster's book *American Film and Society Since 1945* (1991), "Reagan's political 'philosophy' was built around aggressive anticommunism and an antagonism to big government and the welfare state."[3] The new government also debased the anti-war and anti-capitalist movements of the 1960s and 1970s that Hopper personally championed, and scaled back domestic spending on welfare assistance programmes, health care, and income support. Reagan expanded America's nuclear arsenal and military capacity in an effort to confront the Soviet Union under his rigorous spending policy of peace through strength, which was ultimately the flexing of American muscle in the face of an economically weakening Soviet Union. The policy was seen as a success and led to the end of the Cold War and the dismantling of the Soviet Union, leaving America, for good or ill, as the leading economic and militaristic power in the world. Reagan also began a policy of deregulating the banks and supporting free market capitalism, which ushered in "a culture of unbridled greed and materialism—where lining your pocket was the primary goal."[4] It has been argued that this culture of greed saw its pinnacle outcome in the financial crash of 2008 and the subsequent years of austerity that still prevail in some cities in the United States. With such a radical response to post-1960s idealism, it is difficult to comprehend how Dennis Hopper remained a Republican supporter up until just a few weeks before the presidential election of 2008, when he abandoned the Republican Party and publicly backed Democratic nominee Barack Obama for the presidency. The reason for this switch was Republican contender John McCain's choice for running mate, Sarah Palin. He told French journalists: "this time I'll vote for Obama. I was the first person in my family to have been Republican. For most of my life, I wasn't on the Left. I pray God Barack Obama is elected."[5] His prayers were answered, and Barack Obama won the election by 52.9%. It is intriguing to try and understand Hopper's decision to elope to the Republican Party in the first place, when one recalls his role and relationship within 1960s liberalism. Hopper admits: "The idea of less government, more individual freedom, is something that I liked. I started believing it. So I started voting. I voted that time for Reagan..."[6] Hopper's decision seemed to be based on an idea he'd read from Thomas Jefferson that in order for the republic to work, "every 25 years you needed to have change if you are really going to have a republic, and the Democrats had been in power too long."[7] In fact, this statement from Hopper does not entirely ring true. Certainly the Democrats had been in power throughout the 1960s with the administrations of John F. Kennedy and Lyndon B. Johnson respectively. But the only Democratic government to serve during the 1970s was Jimmy Carter, and his administration lasted for only one four-year term. Theoretically, after years of drug and alcohol addiction, Hopper, suddenly clean and sober, saw what he was blind to before. The 1960s utopia of free love and peace had crumbled into an 1980s nightmare of self-indulgence and greed. Members of Hopper's generation had either been swept aside or the stoners and peaceniks had switched sides and were now the CEOs of America's major corporations making big money in Reagan's America and living what was now deemed to be the American Dream.

Capitalism, Republicanism and its grating relationship with 1960s idealism is a theme that is explored in the comedy film *Flashback* (1990), a mash-up of *Easy Rider, Midnight Run* (1988), and *Trading Places* (1983). Hopper plays 1960s activist and now fugitive hippie Huey Walker. The film, is set at the beginning of the 1990s, takes a swipe at the Reagan era of free enterprise and capitalist greed but also comments on the 1960s generation who sold it out. After thirty years on the run for a childish stunt which involved embarrassing then Vice President Spiro Agnew, Huey Walker (who shares the same tousled long hair, bushy beard, and fidgety mannerisms that defined Billy's erratic look in *Easy Rider*) hands himself in to the police and is arrested. Slick FBI agent John Buckner (Kiefer Sutherland) escorts Walker via train to face trial for his past crime. Whilst eating dinner in the train's restaurant carriage, Walker tricks Agent Buckner into thinking he has spiked his food with LSD. After Walker convinces Agent Buckner into drinking copious amounts of tequila to counter the effects of the LSD,

Buckner passes out drunk in his train compartment. Walker shaves off his shaggy beard, cuts his long hair into a short crop, and switches clothes with Agent Buckner. When they arrive for a layover stop in a small town, Walker, taking on Agent Buckner's FBI role, hands over a drunken Agent Buckner to the local sheriff. Whilst Agent Buckner stews in the town jail, Walker takes a stroll and ends up in a bar where two middle-aged, middle-class males are drinking lots of beer and reminiscing about the good old days of the 1960s and the weirdness of the 1980s. Walker starts up a conversation with them about their rebel credentials and asks if they remember the 1960s activist Huey Walker. He informs them that Huey Walker has been caught by the FBI and is rotting in the jail across the street. The two ex-hippies are furious. Walker plays up to his new image of sharp-suited agent and mocks them, delivering the line: "It takes more than going down to your local video store and renting *Easy Rider* to be a rebel," to which one of them replies "I happen to own *Easy Rider*." When Agent Buckner wakes up in the jail, he insists that the sheriff has made a grave mistake. The sheriff ignores his pleas and allows a fellow drunk jail occupant to give Buckner a beating on the grounds that he is a draft dodger. When the local police officers check Walker's file, they realise there is a huge inconsistency with the age printed on the charge sheet and that of the youthful man in the cell. The sheriff is apologetic but realises that his shady political career is finished if he allows Buckner to leave. The middle-class guys from the bar decide to kidnap Walker (who they still believe is Agent Buckner) and call the local sheriff to arrange a prisoner exchange. When the kidnappers and police meet to exchange, Walker and Agent Buckner agree that the sheriff will try to silence them no matter what. They make an escape and the two foes (personal and generational) become unlikely comrades. By coincidence, Agent Buckner grew up in the local area, and he and Walker traverse the wilderness until they happen upon an old abandoned hippie commune. It turns out that the straight-laced Buckner grew up on the commune as a child. His apparent switch to an unfeeling and cold FBI agent was a response to what he perceived as his parents' failure to grasp reality and take responsibility. By the end of the movie, the roles in which Walker and Buckner played have been switched. Buckner quits the FBI and hits the road on a motorcycle in a quest for freedom, whilst Walker, sharp-suited and loaded with cash from his autobiography sales (his capture was a publicity stunt instigated by himself to generate sales of his book), cruises round town in a private limo, claiming capitalism is the way forward and that greed is good.

There is nothing overtly political in content about *Flashback*, yet by casting Dennis Hopper as Huey Walker the movie creates an echo of

Hopper's former 1960s persona. To have the character then turn his back on those ideals is a fitting mirroring of Hopper's own journey towards Republicanism. Moving to the right of the political spectrum did not mean that Hopper lost his sense of what was right and wrong in terms of cultural and social justice. Reagan's arrival into office meant that Hollywood's era of protest and social commentary came to a somewhat abrupt end. The otherwise liberal players in Hollywood were sidelined in favour of big budget action flicks with unethical uses of corporate and militaristic power and lack of responsibility to others. The book *Hollywood's New Radicalism* quotes *One Flew Over the Cuckoo's Nest* cinematographer Haskell Wexler's description of the typical Hollywood movie as guides to "screw each other over, kill each other and rip each other off".[8] A number of films did sneak under the radar of conservative Hollywood and wedged themselves between the 1980s capitalist propaganda that Hollywood studios were churning out. Among these films was Oliver Stone's *Wall Street* (1986), a critical assessment of corporate greed and immoral trading, and also Stone's *Salvador* (1986), a damming look at America's intrusion into Latin American politics. Another standout was Hopper's own *Colors* (1988). Although on the surface, *Colors* is a film that works like a documentary of the Black-American and Latino gangs of Los Angeles, it also represents a deeper problem inflicted upon urban youth by Reagan's policies. In 1983, the administration made drastic cuts to the federal fund for employment training that was seen as a lifeline for urban youth to better themselves and step outside of their troubled neighbourhoods. These cuts left poor and predominantly Black-American youths stranded and reliant on drugs, theft, guns, and violence to get by. Albert Auster and Leonard Quart argue that:

> During the Reagan years many of the black economic and social gains of the 1960s and 1970s, ranging from the rate of college attendance to the proportion of two parent families to relative income levels, began to decline while poverty and crime rates escalated.[9]

The youths found family and community ties within gang culture. *Colors* is an analytical representation and a reflection of the policies inflicted upon black communities in the 1980s by the Reagan administration. Hopper's decision to shift the original screenplay's focus of drugs to gang culture and to change the location from Chicago to Los Angeles produced one of the most politically potent films of the 1980s. The fact that Hopper was a Republican backer at the time was something of a moot point.

Political commentary in Hopper's filmography after 2000 was relatively non-existent—a shame, considering the administration of George W. Bush was ripe for satirical take-downs or more blatant criticism. Filmmaker Michael Moore's documentaries *Bowling for Columbine* (2002), *Fahrenheit 9/11* (2004), and *Sicko* (2007) provided sensationalism and criticism of the Bush administration's policies on gun control, terrorism, foreign policy, and health care respectively. Television shows such as *The West Wing* (1999-2006) provided a satirical take on government during a time of serious public repercussions after 9/11. Director George Romero always included subtle political commentary throughout his films. According to some film critics and historians, the 'zombie carnage' of Romero's first film *Night of the Living Dead* (1968) "seemed a grotesque echo of the conflict then raging in Vietnam."[10] *Easy Rider* takes much credit for defining the conflicts of the 1960s, but Romero's "*...of the Dead*" series of films document far more bluntly the divisions in American society. In 2005, Hopper appeared in Romero's *Land of the Dead* as Paul Kaufman, a corrupt leader of a gated and secure high-rise community called Fiddlers Green. The zombie apocalypse has decimated the Earth, but Fiddlers Green remains an untouched and modern skyscraper setting "where the wealthy can live in hermetically sealed luxury".[11] When one of the zombie hoard, referred to as Big Daddy, begins a march on Fiddlers Green, amassing a zombie following along the way, Kaufman sends out an armed unit to smash the rebellion. Romero referred to *Land of the Dead* as an "attempt to explore the post 9/11 mentality, and that Kaufman's administration of Fiddlers Green could be seen as analogous to the presidential administration of George W. Bush."[12] As someone who openly admitted he voted for Bush "father and son", *Land of the Dead* becomes a subversive film for Hopper to be a part of. First, Hopper is playing what we perceive as a credible leader and an authority figure that blows apart his anti-authority status of the 1960s. Kaufman is powerful, smart, wealthy, and despises anybody who is under his class status. Kaufman has created a class system within Fiddlers Green. The 'upper-class' live within the luxury of the city-sized building; below, the 'middle-class' consist of those brave enough to protect and surround the monolithic building, and outside of the compound are the 'underclass', the zombies, left to their own devices. Second, Hopper is given lines that directly imitate those of George W. Bush. For example, in one pivotal scene Kaufman proclaims: "We do not negotiate with terrorists"—a statement the Bush administration repeatedly used in its War on Terror propaganda push. Kaufman also sees his troops as disposable: he sends them on deadly errands and orders them to quash the zombie hoard. They are worth risking in order to protect his privileged way of life and that of his class—a shrewd conception of the Bush administration's careless deployment of troops in Iraq.

As the 2008 presidential campaign approached, Hopper lent his acting chops to two films that dealt a blow to the left from the Hollywood right, represented by Kelsey Grammer and Jon Voight's hawkish politics. The film *An American Carol* (*2008*) was unapologetically crass and featured an ensemble cast of right-wing conservatives, from Grammer and Voight to Lesley Neilson and James Woods, mocking the Hollywood left. The film particularly took aim at filmmaker Michael Moore—here disguised as Michael Malone and played by comic actor Kevin Farley. Using the narrative framework of Charles Dickens' *A Christmas Carol,* Malone is visited by three spirits of an American past, present, and future. Hopper's role as Judge Clarence Henderson was thankfully just one scene, but his involvement was the big issue, especially in the subtext of 1960s idealism. His scene involves an invasion of his courtroom by lawyers of the American Civil Liberties Union (ACLU), portrayed as infected zombies. Henderson gleefully hoists a shotgun and takes out the ACLU zombies. Founded in 1920, the ACLU won many victories for minority groups. During the social upheaval of the 1960s, they represented cases in fields such as gay rights, abortion rights, and racial discrimination and segregation. Hopper alluded to the ACLU in *Easy Rider* with the introduction of Jack Nicholson's character George Hanson, a likable yet drunkard lawyer who had also "done a lot of work for the ACLU". He meets Billy and Wyatt in jail whilst recovering from a heavy drinking bender and in reference to Billy and Wyatt's shabby appearance explains to them that "they used rusty razor blades on the last two long hairs they brought in here, and I wasn't here to protect um". Hanson helps the pair get out of jail without too much trouble, making him a saviour of not only Billy and Wyatt but of all marginalised peoples. Hopper's aligning with the hawks of republicanism in *An American Carol* and denouncing the left agenda, past and present is, in itself, quite shocking.

The comedy drama *Swing Vote* (2008) saw Hopper teamed up again with Kelsey Grammer and his *Waterworld* co-star Kevin Costner. The film's premise of an election decided by the vote of one ordinary man allowed left and right to play off against one another in comedic circumstances. Grammer's character, the Republican incumbent president Andrew Boone, vies for Costner's vote against Hopper's democratic nominee, Donald Greenleaf. Although the film tries to show the ever-shifting policies of the left and right to achieve votes and gain popularity, the fact that two Republican backers played the central roles was telling. Hopper's Greenleaf is sentimental and dippy, whilst Boone is hawkish. The clichés are absolute. However, *Swing*

Vote should be considered a turning point for Hopper. His performance in the film was subject to a number of editorial cuts, much to Hopper's dismay, which dispensed with a character-defining subplot. In a number of promotional interviews, Hopper criticised the film, stating that: "My subplot was completely cut. There's a scene we shot where I ditch all my events to go support a young Mexican waitress at the funeral of her grandfather. It was chopped. It was important to the development of my character and it's missing."[13] The scene itself is included on the DVD extras of *Swing Vote,* and although the scene did not fit well within the light, comedic context of *Swing Vote,* Hopper does deliver a strong speech which, if it had been incorporated into the film, might have provided his character with far more credence. Kelsey Grammer was also subject to a similar cut in which he is seen conversing with Native Americans and receives a dramatic visit from his animal spirit guide, a huge elephant, the symbol of the Republican Party.

With the advent of Barack Obama, Hopper's decision to return to his Democratic roots was not difficult to fathom. So many people in America had become reinvigorated with American politics by Obama's charm, optimism, and proposal for change in American society. People saw in Obama a fresh approach to foreign policy, a set of values and ideals that harked back to the civil rights movement, and a passing political resemblance to the aspiration and change that John F. Kennedy and his brother Robert F. Kennedy once promoted. In response to Obama's rise, McCain's campaign and the conservative media could only conjure up often race-based allegations of Obama's ancestry and birthplace, his acquaintance with proposed radicals, and his religious orientation. Paired with Sarah Palin's unease and inexperience in handling one-on-one interviews with seasoned political commentators, the right began to look outdated and irrelevant. Hopper's decision to switch allegiances in the early 1980s was based on his assumption that the nominees had America's best interests at heart. Hopper, after all, was always an American patriot who was critical of America when required yet also vocally supportive. For all his apparent faults in domestic policy, Ronald Reagan boosted the American economy, ushered in an era of unprecedented growth and prosperity, and accelerated peace negotiations to bring an end to the lengthy Cold War with the Soviet Union.

Dennis Hopper's switch to the right ties in with a bigger picture of conventional American values versus 1960s idealism that is presented in Joseph Heath and Andrew Potter's book *The Rebel Sell: Why the Culture Can't be Jammed.* Heath and Potter's notion that "any act that violates conventional social norms is politically radical" encompasses the positional ideology of the counter-culture rebel, and particularly the belief that this behaviour is "such a profound threat to the established order that it must be suppressed at any cost". From this standpoint, Hopper's countercultural milestone *Easy Rider* could not allow its protagonists Billy and Wyatt to live because the "freedom represented by the two bikers—the drugs, the long hair, the choppers on the open road—is intolerable to the status quo".[15] Even those loosely associated with them—such as ACLU hero George Hanson—has to die, because America was, and still is, a deeply conformist and structured society. Hopper's conservatism and patriotism was on display well before he began voting Republican. In a 1972 interview with *Gallery*, Hopper poignantly expressed his concerns:

> I look at America today and I really wonder how much longer a society like ours can exist. How much longer can we have wars, how much longer can we keep raising our national debt and shaking our missiles before it all falls apart? What's wrong with the country is that we've forgotten how we started, which was to have a government of the people, by the people, and for the people—and that the people then have to approve and support that government.[16]

Whilst this interview took place in 1972, Hopper could have been talking about contemporary America. Hopper may have backed the wrong side in a government that has increasingly become less about the people and more about supporting big business and external conflicts. Yet Hopper always seemed aware of America's deep-rooted problems and remained adamant that a better America could be fought for—on the left or the right.

Love and Hate

The Conflict of Emotions in *The Blackout* and *Carried Away*

Dennis Hopper was never a typical leading man. His edgy movements, abrupt hysterical voice, and menacing stare were enough to frighten even the most depraved objects of his character's desires. In his analysis of Hopper's career, film critic Adrian Martin describes Hopper as "short, no neck, square, and solid, a little beefy, but still quite handsome…".[1] Although certainly handsome in his youth and later a somewhat distinguished older gentleman with a mischievous glint in his eye, "short", "square", and "a little beefy" were hardly the desired look of a leading man. Hopper ranks among a group of actors—mostly those designated as character actors—whose mannerisms and looks are too strange for the role of the romantic lead. If they are cast in such a position, then they often mutate into the menacing, bleeding heart of love and infatuation: in Hopper's case, the obsessive controller in *Blue Velvet,* the abusive drunken husband in *Eye of the Storm* (1991), the pitying simpleton in *Held to Ransom* (2000), the outcast weirdo in *The River's Edge*, the outspoken and controlling egotist in *Search and Destroy* (1995), or the compulsive killer in *Speed.* Love, or perhaps romantic love, rarely plays a crucial part. Martin observes that "Sex scenes are strikingly rare in his filmography, and tend to be deliberately perverse or shocking…".[2] This phenomenon is witnessed from *Tracks* to *Blue Velvet* and beyond. Rarely is a sex scene carried out with tenderness and caring. That being said, nestled within his extensive catalogue of films is *Carried Away* (1996, also released as *Acts of Love*), a tale of love and tenderness in the throes of middle age and the search for excitement and joy within the confines of a tired relationship. *Carried Away* sticks out like a blackened thumb in Hopper's film work, if only for the fact that his character is for all intents and purposes the romantic hero of the piece, a claim that cannot be awarded to most, if any, of Hopper's output. However, the film is threaded with a dark underbelly of jealousy and a loss of innocence that shimmers just underneath the quaint surface. The film's tenderness is poisoned by a bitter love triangle that transforms the lives of those involved. This premise is strangely mirrored in *The Blackout* (1997), although the dark underbelly that lies within *The Blackout* is disturbingly brought to the surface. The two films are polar opposite in terms of tone and content, but it is credit to Hopper that he somehow weaves an evocative thread between two such contrasting films.

New York director Abel Ferrara's films explore themes of responsibility, guilt, and internal conflict. The protagonists of his movies are often the cause of their own dilemmas. In his commercial peak of the 1990s, Ferrara explored themes of redemption and redress. For example, *King of New York* (1990) follows the exploits of mob boss Frank White (Christopher Walken) and his attempt to go straight and to use his influence and power ultimately for the good of the people, although many bad deeds come to pass before this is achieved. Ferrara followed this film with notions of Catholic guilt by way of Harvey Keitel's wayward and corrupt *Bad Lieutenant* (1992), who begins to seek redemption from his perverse life when a nun is raped by two youths. Ferrara's films feel aggressive, dirty, and sleazy but always absolutely vital. Ferrara's background as a director of cheap porn films such as *9 Lives of a Wet Pussy* (1976) and trashy video nasties like *Driller Killer* (1979) have remnants in his modern films. The grainy film stock, later switching to gritty digital film and handheld camera motion, perfectly captures Ferrara's stories in a highly realistic manner. *The Blackout* is no exception. As both these films are relatively obscure, I provide below an in-depth analysis of the story. It was important to do this in order to provide evidence of the two films' narrative links.

The Blackout revolves around Matty (Matthew Modine), a Hollywood film star who is fuelled on drugs, booze, fame, and his own inflamed ego. During some downtime from filming, he visits his fiancée Annie (Beatrice Dalle, referred to in the screenplay as Annie 1) in Miami and embarks on a drug, drink, and sex-fuelled odyssey with local video artist, filmmaker, club owner, and general sleaze ball Mickey Wayne (Dennis Hopper). Mickey owns a sex club/art/film studio in which his clients pay to be filmed by a team of video artists engaging in all kinds of weird sex with the numerous dancers and prostitutes who work the club. Mickey informs Matty that Annie has agreed to star in a movie he is making, a lowbrow and highly sexed-up remake of director Dorothy Arzner's 1934 film *Nana*. Although Matty has taken time out from filmmaking, he is now unwittingly partaking in another film of Mickey's making.

Matty and Annie 1 spend the night at the club and share a passionate dance in front of the club's patrons, whilst in the shadows Mickey films them. In the early hours, Matty and Annie return to their apartment a little worse for wear. Annie reveals to Matty that she has recently had an abortion and proclaims she does not want a junkie to be the father of her child. Visibly upset, Matty trashes the room and Annie storms out, leaving a voice mail playing a previous drug-induced rant from Matty about how he would like to cut the baby from her body. Matty slumps down, listening to his own drugged-out confession.

The next evening, Matty returns to Mickey's club, looking for Annie 1. The two embark on an even more heinous drug spree. They visit the apartment of two local prostitutes and take copious amounts of drugs and liquor. The night turns sour when Matty becomes far too smashed for sex or anything else. He stumbles out of the prostitute's apartment in the early hours of the morning. As the sun rises, he wanders into a small coffee shop and begins a conversation with a young waitress, who also happens to be called Annie (Sarah Lassez, referred to in the screenplay as Annie 2). Although he is stoned out of his mind and looking like death warmed up, she recognises him. She tells him she wants to become an actress as well. He takes Annie 2 back to the club to meet Mickey. Mickey is in his edit suite piecing together footage of the dance between Matty and Annie 1 from the previous evening. Matty introduces Annie 2 to Mickey. Matty sees the video footage on the screen of his ex-fiancé and reacts emotionally, crying, kissing, and crawling up to the screen. Mickey takes Annie 2 back into a costume room where he films her trying on wigs. Mickey picks out a short black wig for her to wear, which resembles Annie 1's short and sleek hairstyle. Mickey leads her back out into the edit suite, his camera still rolling. An emotional Matty sees Annie 2, and in his drug-fuelled stupor believes her to be his ex-fiancé. He begins sobbing and with Mickey's encouragement starts kissing and groping at her. Up until this point, Annie 2 has believed Matty to be acting, but she soon realises that not all is right and becomes noticeably frightened. The scene abruptly ends.

The narrative jumps forward eighteen months. Matty is now clean and sober, living in New York, and in a much calmer relationship with Susan (Claudia Schiffer), a visual artist. Matty begins to have flashbacks and terrible dreams relating to that fateful night in Miami. Unable to understand why this is happening, he seeks out a therapist (played by Ferrara). During one session, he tells the therapist about a recurring dream that seems all too real. In the dream, he is throttling his ex-fiancée. Whilst Susan has some business to attend to out of town, Matty decides that he must seek out the truth of what happened and elicit some sort of closure. He heads back to Miami and finds Mickey Wayne on the beach, cavorting with some bikini-clad girls. Matty pleads with Mickey to help him track down Annie 1. Mickey informs him that she has long gone, happily married and living in New Mexico. Matty insists he needs to talk with Annie 1 and after a while, Mickey agrees reluctantly to make some contacts and promises to let Matty know when he has news. Returning to his hotel, Matty is unable to endure the wait and begins to empty the mini bar contents, downing each little bottle of spirits in one swift shot.

The next morning he is abruptly woken by a knock on the door. Mickey and Annie 1 walk into the room and discover Matty sprawled out on the floor, severely wasted and surrounded by empty bottles. Matty attempts to speak to Annie 1 but cannot string a sentence together. She leaves with Mickey, any chance of resolution lost. Matty spends the rest of the day drinking and cannot even pretend to be sober when he receives a phone call from a worried Susan who has returned to New York. He informs her that he has fallen off the wagon but will return that night. Susan insists she come out to Miami and collect him. He refuses and repeats that he will return to New York. On the drive back to the airport, he sits restlessly in the back seat of his chauffeur-driven car. Instead of going home, Matty reaffirms his conviction to find out the truth of what happened eighteen months ago. He proceeds to the club and in the edit suite begins to watch the video that Mickey shot the night of his blackout. On screen, Annie 2 enters the room, wearing the short black wig. The scene plays out as before, but this time we see a strung-out and emotional Matty force himself upon a confused and scared Annie 2. Matty watches in horror as the blanks from that night are filled in before his eyes. He breaks down as he watches himself crush his hands around Annie 2's neck and strangle her to death. The video ends. Matty weeps uncontrollably by the flickering screen. Mickey approaches from the darkness of the club and watches Matty crying before scolding him for being such a drugged-up waste of space. He demands that Matty get out of his club, shouting and ranting until Matty finally runs out. Under the darkness of night, Matty stumbles across an empty beach, still sobbing. He begins to wander out into the waves of the ocean. Suddenly, Susan appears, running across the sand. Matty confesses to her what he has done, pushes her away, and runs back into the waves. Before she can follow, Matty has already disappeared out of sight. She slumps down onto the sand as the waves break. Matty is last seen being embraced by the spirit of the girl he murdered.

The Blackout is a film of parallels, including the two Annies and Mickey and Matty. Moreover, it is impossible to watch Dennis Hopper's performance and not draw comparisons with *Blue Velvet's* Frank Booth. The character of Mickey Wayne could almost be an older Frank if he had survived the gunshot to the head. However, while Mickey is something of a sleaze, he also considers himself a creative artist, a characteristic that could not be pinned on Frank Booth. His club and facilities bear some resemblance to Andy Warhol's art studio, The Factory. The place is populated by beautiful women, sleazy movie stars, musicians, and hangers-on, all with enough cash to participate in the sordid activities that go on in the establishment.

Incidentally, in the early to mid-1960s, Hopper himself happened to be one of those movie stars who found themselves embroiled in Warhol's art scene. He developed a working friendship with Warhol, appearing in Warhol's silent film portraits *Screen Tests* (1964-1966). Furthermore, Mickey Wayne demonstrates an emotion Frank Booth is incapable of: guilt.

When a cleaned-up Matty returns to Miami eighteen months later to try to unravel the mystery of his disturbing dreams, he finds Mickey on the beach with a troupe of young girls inexplicably dancing in bikinis for him. Mickey cannot hide his displeasure at seeing Matty again. Although Mickey ultimately helps him trace Annie 1, it is obvious that he would prefer Matty to disappear and never return. The reason for Mickey's reaction is explained later when Matty pays a visit to his editing suite and watches the video, shot by Mickey, of him and Annie 2. As Matty realises what he did that night, he can barely contain his anguish. Mickey stands back and berates him for being an over-privileged junkie. Although he is angry at Matty for the death of Annie 2, he is equally angry with himself for being an accomplice. In a forceful monologue, he sums up his disgust with Matty but also his disgust with himself. The pace and volume of the monologue intensifies as Mickey slowly loses his patience with Matty's behaviour:

> What kind of piece of shit are you? What kind of piece of fucking filth are you? You big fucking movie star. Come down and shit all over my parade brother, you big over-privileged movie star. You killed that fucking chick that night and I watched you, and I don't fucking wanna cop out on this and say hey man but I didn't know she was fucking dead till I touched her fucking face. And you couldn't have possibly known she was dead because you had some sort of fucking blackout man. I got rid of her, got rid of her! When are you fucking going to take responsibility, look in the fucking mirror and grow up, motherfucker, grow up real fucking quick cause you're not going to live very long, cause this is my life too you piece of shit. Fuck you and the fucking horse you rode in on. You get out of my fucking life; you get out of my fucking life, out of my fucking mind, out of my fucking memory.

In terms of the 'fuck' usage, the monologue is reminiscent of some of Frank Booth's torrents of rage. However, what singles this particular monologue out is Mickey's own desire to forget, and his own sense of wrongdoing, which prevents him from being able to forget. The return of Matty unlocks Mickey's own repressed memories and emotions regarding that night, his own guilt at not having stopped Matty and continuing to film the episode, knowing Matty's sanity had long gone. It is a truly authentic moment. Here, Hopper distils the essence of Mickey's rage, the pure horror of the reality of that night. To theorise, perhaps Hopper was able to find a connection to that rage in his own troubled past, which is why this monologue stands out the way it does. Matthew Modine's character of Matty in many ways resembles a younger Dennis Hopper, not in looks or characteristics but in circumstance and place. The younger Hopper, full of talent, ambition, and praise from the industry and his peers was stalled by drugs, ego, and a sense of self-importance. His early promise, at least by Hollywood's standards, was shattered. In this moment, one can picture an older but no less damaged Hopper, with earned maturity and experience, call to account his younger, arrogant, and wasteful self. It is a significant moment of catharsis, an opportunity to purge and reveal hidden truths, not just about the characters in the film but also about himself as an actor and as an individual.

There are scenes in this film that show Dennis Hopper to be an extremely versatile actor, with a great sense of depth and understanding for the role of Mickey Wayne and also for those actors around him. As is often the case, Hopper's desire, intentional or otherwise, to fill the screen with his presence can often overwhelm the whole movie. In *The Blackout,* he allows his co-stars to take centre stage while he merges with the background. For example, when Mickey and Matty visit the prostitute's apartment, they proceed to snort cocaine and Mickey once again takes out his video camera to capture the moment as the two prostitutes start kissing and fondling each other. They begin to undress a stoned and almost incapacitated Matty. Mickey joins in, inspecting one of the prostitutes up close, spreading her legs and rubbing his hand between her thighs. He offers an extravagant hand gesture whilst also sticking his tongue out in a grubby sneer. This act never pulls our focus away from what Matty is experiencing, in fact it adds surrealism to his already nightmarish experience. During the promotional run for *Elegy* (2008), Dennis Hopper appeared on many television chat shows proclaiming his co-star Sir Ben Kingsley to be a generous and giving actor. This generosity may be true of Kingsley, but it is also true of Dennis Hopper. Adrian Martin points out that: "One endlessly enthralling sign of Hopper's skill is his ability to listen to other actors who share a scene with him. How he registers this is silent reaction shots".[3] This is apparent in *The Blackout* with his interactions with Matty. In Mickey Wayne, Hopper found an outlet for some of his extreme tendencies, and although he attempts to keep it low key in places, you can see Hopper relish the sleazy antics of Mickey Wayne, and as viewers, we savour it with him. Interestingly, Howard Hampton observes that *The Blackout* is:

> packed with more insight into art/obsession/addiction/self-destruction than all of Hopper's directing efforts combined: it is as if this is the kind of film Hopper would have directed had he been really able to commit himself to his material.[4]

It is undoubtedly a provocative point, and certainly, there are aspects of Hopper's artistic and cultural interests present within the film. However, Hopper's artistic life goes beyond the mere direction of a film. His whole life resembles an artistic act of "art/obsession/addiction/self-destruction".

Although *The Blackout* predates our volatile era of media intrusions and celebrity obsession only by a year or so (the internet being in its infancy at the time the film was released), the film functions as a dramatic critique of the celebrity lifestyle and eerily highlights a future where media personalities are allowed, even encouraged, to wallow in obnoxious self- worth. Matty is a typical hard-living hedonist, abusing drugs and drink to the limits with his rich and disconnected friends. It is this disconnect from reality that leads to some of the film's most dramatic and disturbing scenes. The video cameras that follow Matty around the club and later into the prostitute's apartment are symbolic of a life lived through the lens; the ever-prying eye constantly deconstructing personality and behaviour. Matty is so immune to the camera that he no longer masks his emotions but wildly indulges in shocking behaviour in front of the camera. The only outsider from the celebrity circle that Matty inhabits is Annie 2. As her time is spent in Matty's company, her naiveté is exploited, she is led astray and corrupted and eventually abused and killed. Her life means nothing to Matty until over a year later, when he is sober and guilt-ridden that he may have actually hurt Annie 1. Annie 2 is disposed of by Mickey after Matty becomes so incapable and intoxicated that he suffers a blackout. Annie 2's undignified body disposal demonstrates how insignificant she was as a person. To Matty and Mickey, Annie 2 was simply a plaything. *The Blackout* dramatically invokes an image of celebrity that belittles those outside of the circle and yet encourages people to still desire that lifestyle.

The Blackout is an exhilarating if uncomfortable film. Its characters live what they perceive to be the American Dream of money, beauty, fame, fast cars, and sex. On the one hand they have it all, yet on the other hand it is the sinister flip side of the American Dream: drugs, drink, scandal, and egotism all spiralling into madness and paranoia. There are not many filmmakers who can display such fear, loathing, and sleaze on screen quite like Abel Ferrara. His movies are marked with the grime of the city streets they inhabit. *The Blackout* offers a trip into a dark and base world, inhabited by sadistic people in search of cheap thrills.

Dennis Hopper's performance in *Carried Away* (1996) is not one that audiences would have expected, especially at this point in his career. Hopper's regular stints as wailing madmen, stoners, or drunks had rendered the misconception that Hopper was unable to achieve subtlety. *Carried Away* is a restrained, quiet film—one might venture the opinion that the film is whimsical in its approach. In a review, *The New York Times* remarked that *Carried Away* was "self-consciously high-minded",[5] and this is plausible as it struggles with the grand themes of love, loss, and lust explored in the narrative. Nevertheless, the film shimmers with moments of brilliance.

The story concerns Joseph, a forty-seven-year-old school teacher who has lived his entire life in the same rural town, working at the same school. He has been in love with Rosealea (Amy Irving) his whole life, though she had once been married to his best friend who was killed in the Korean War. Rosealea now teaches alongside Joseph at the local school and lives with her teenage son. Injured as a child in a farming accident, Joseph suffers with a badly damaged leg, needing to walk with the use of a cane. Joseph's life now revolves around the responsibility of taking care of his dying mother, maintaining the remnants of the old family farm, continuing his jaded relationship with Rosealea, and teaching his bored, small-town students. Joseph is coasting though life; content with his lot, but not particularly happy. When new student Katherine (Amy Locane) arrives onto the scene, he is clearly intrigued to see how different she is in comparison to his other students. It is only later when he is introduced to her father, a retired army major (Gary Busey), that their relationship begins to develop. The major asks if Joseph would be willing to stable Katherine's horse. Accepting a fee for the service, Joseph agrees and invites Katherine over anytime to groom and ride the horse. It is in the stable that Joseph and Katherine begin to explore their interest in each other. Their first major encounter is when Joseph finds Katherine unexpectedly sleeping above the stables. He climbs up the ladder and settles down beside her, watching her sleep. To his confusion, she wakes up and pushes her breasts out towards him, proceeding to remove her sweater and revealing her breasts. Joseph panics, gets up, and walks out of the stable, troubled by both the unexpectedness of the moment and his own yearning for it. Crossing the yard, he catches sight of his sickly mother stumbling and coughing inside the house. He pauses and watches her for a moment. He turns back to the stable and climbs up the ladder once again. Katherine is still there, half naked. Joseph suggests that they should make love. Of course, nothing is ever simple when one is embroiled in a love affair with a teenage girl. Already in a relationship with Rosealea, Joseph is torn between the exciting yet inappropriate affair with Katherine and the undemanding, safe yet tiresome relationship with Rosealea. While Joseph genuinely loves Rosealea, their relationship has dragged along for years, never reaching its full potential, with neither Joseph nor Rosealea fully committing.

This indecision begins to tear Joseph apart. Unable to sleep, Joseph has a sudden epiphany and drives over to Rosealea's farm in the middle of a hard rainstorm. Once there, he reveals his desire to change the way he lives and demands that Rosealea does the same, which is, essentially to stop living as a sad widow and fully commit to being his partner and lover. Joseph expresses his desire to go and see the ocean for the first time in his life or to visit New York City. He tells her that for once he wants to make love to her with the lights on and insists that she respond to him with the same passion she once had for her deceased husband. He begins to strip off his clothes, turning on all the lights in the dining room as he does so. This scene that Hopper shares with actress Amy Irving is particularly striking simply because it is so unexpected within the confines of the film's narrative. As Joseph strips naked in front of Rosealea, she becomes so overwhelmed by his honesty that she retreats to the kitchen. After taking a steadying breath and a quick drink for courage, she begins to remove her dress whilst in the background Joseph takes a seat. This is a great dual acting moment, a scene in which both actors seem to be reacting to each other without being in the same room. Whilst Rosealea nervously undresses in the darkened foreground, Joseph, through the kitchen doorway, sits down on the couch reassuringly rubbing his naked arms and silently cursing to himself. She eventually comes through in just her underwear and takes a huge unsteady gulp of whiskey before finally removing all her clothing and standing naked in front of Joseph, as if for the very first time. They embrace, kissing, and begin to make love on the dining room floor. It is an excellent, tender moment from two senior actors who share a sincere, if not overly passionate, on-screen chemistry. Interestingly, the sex scenes involving Katherine do not share the same level of intimacy.

This moment of honesty, however, does not break the ties that Joseph has with Katherine. After one particularly potent sexual encounter, the two lie in the hayloft, fast asleep. The local doctor (Hal Halbrook), who is at the farm treating Joseph's mother, wanders into the barn and catches the sleeping couple. Although Joseph later meets the doctor in a bar in an attempt to explain himself and his actions, it is at this point in the story that their secret begins to unravel.

Joseph's mother passes away and the funeral brings many well-wishers to his home and cards of condolences. One card happens to come from Katherine, who writes about how she wants to make love in the house now that his mother is gone. Rosealea opens this card and confronts Joseph outside the barn. Joseph is remorseful of his actions. Rosealea pushes him and storms out of the wake. After the wake is over, Joseph proceeds to get blind drunk and crashes out on the living room floor. Later that evening, Katherine arrives at Joseph's house and finds him the worse for wear. Nevertheless, she heads upstairs to Joseph's room and strips naked, determined to continue her juvenile fantasy. Joseph slowly follows her and attempts to explain to Katherine that he is torn: he cares about her, but he also loves Rosealea. When Katherine naively continues her seduction attempt, Joseph pushes her away saying she could not understand his situation, implying her immaturity. She stops, and tells him that he will be sorry. Katherine leaves the house, clearly upset and angered by Joseph's rejection. Joseph then goes to Rosealea's house, attempting, whilst drunk, to explain his actions. Unable to make sense of his feelings, he crashes on her couch and proceeds to pass out.

Days later at the schoolhouse, Rosealea's vengeful teenage son Robert tells Joseph that the major knows about his relationship with Katherine and is making plans to come and see him. Returning home, Joseph loads his hunting rifle expecting trouble from the major. He anxiously hides out in the barn and waits until nightfall. When the major and his inebriated wife pull up in his driveway, Joseph points the gun at them, urging them to leave him alone. In Joseph's mind, an ex-army officer would probably want him dead for seducing his innocent daughter, though the reverse is true, but the major only wants to discuss the situation. They go inside the farmhouse and the major informs Joseph that he would be crazy to even consider a future with his daughter, who he sees as being extremely immature, and that for Joseph's own sake he should be the one to end the relationship. Joseph confesses to not having a great deal of experience with such matters. The major's wife, already drunk, suddenly becomes aggressive and verbally abuses Joseph. Embarrassed, the major ends the conversation and escorts his wife back home. As the major leaves, Katherine appears in the back entrance saying that her father told her that Joseph was never serious about their relationship. She pleads with him not to end it and suggests they could just simply remain lovers. When Joseph reassures her that it is for the best that they part, she innocently proclaims she has done something bad and points towards the barn outside which is now ablaze. Joseph runs out and desperately tries to free the horses from inside the burning barn. He does so, but as Katherine's horse runs from the barn, its coat catches fire. Katherine runs after her horse as the barn—the scene of their lovemaking—collapses. Joseph finds Katherine sitting by the corpse of her beloved horse.

The next day whilst looking over the charred remains of his barn, Joseph realises that there is now nothing keeping him trapped in his hometown. His farm has burnt down, his mother has passed away, and his relationship with Katherine has ended. He collects all the coins he has been saving for years and begins to count them out on the kitchen table. He visits Rosealea and they have a sincere discussion, admitting that they have both let each other down. Joseph explains his desire to live a more fulfilling life while he still can. With their feelings renewed and with a new sense of purpose for the future, they leave together, and for the first time ever Joseph sees the ocean. Rosealea walks into the waves whilst Joseph at first seems hesitant to step into the water. He stands in the waves letting the water roll across his feet. He eventually joins Rosealea and they stand together in the surf.

Carried Away and *The Blackout* both explore themes of passion, showing two extreme sides of the same coin. One side is tender and loving though prone to temptation, the other is dark and disturbing and indulges temptation in all its forms. It is Hopper's triumph that he can portray these very subtle differences between love and hate, sex and anger, tenderness and brutality. In *The Blackout*, Hopper's character, Mickey Wayne, is depraved yet not emotionally cut off. In *Carried Away*, his character Joseph is caring but disconnected from the world around him. Both men do things that are wrong, perhaps even viewed as perverted, and this is certainly true in the case of Mickey, but both accept the consequences of their actions. In *The Blackout*, Mickey is both instigator and witness, and in essence, an accomplice to a young girl's murder. The blending of sex and violence in an uncontrolled and permissive environment is ultimately what leads to her death. And in *Carried Away* Joseph enters into a consensual sexual relationship with a seventeen-year-old student. This relationship with Katherine ultimately triggers the destruction of her own self-delusions but launches Joseph out of his stale and disappointing life and into the world. Both characters are guilty in some way for the loss of a young girl's innocence. Mickey is clearly the more extreme of the two, but they both make the same decisions with far-reaching consequences. Joseph at first tries to deny his impulses but eventually gives in to Katherine's seduction. Mickey, on the other hand, never denies himself a thrill. Hopper's on-screen portrayal of love and passion has always been intense, often bordering on obsession and possession. His character's desire to conquer and to own the object of their affections has been witnessed in many films. In *Blue Velvet*, he beats, berates, and even kidnaps the husband and son of Dorothy Vallens in order to secure her devotion and sexual enslavement. In *River's Edge*, his character Feck was once so in love that killing the girl of his dreams seemed the only way he could prove it, and ultimately he seems proud to brag about it to the local kids. In a much more distressing context, the love, or lust, he feels for his daughter CeeBee in *Out of the Blue* crosses over into actual incest and sexual abuse. However intense these emotions are, there is also a sense—again, with the exception of *Carried Away*—that when it comes to the expression of love and sexual desire, Hopper's characters are complete and utter failures. Frank Booth is such a ball of pent-up sexual aggression that only the weirdest, twisted acts get him excited. When he finally climaxes in *Blue Velvet,* it is only by dry humping Dorothy's velvet robe, and even this appears only as an internal orgasm. In *Tracks*, he takes a beautiful girl he meets on the train to a windswept meadow, where they roll around like young teenagers. However, when he begins to get rough, she throws him off, and he runs away weeping. In *The Blackout*, Hopper becomes a voyeur of live sex shows. His hand-held digital video camera captures everything, including the murder of Annie 2; however, he is never a participant in these acts, only a lurid observer. Hopper stated that

> sex, hate, love. These things are very powerful tools to be able to utilise and put into our work. I think it's important to know who we are and what we're about, and we'll find trouble inside us, and that will come out and we'll express that in our films.[6]

Love and sex are certainly complicated; in the characters that Dennis Hopper portrays, these acts and emotions are almost impossible without some inner turmoil at the centre of the character. However, with the characters of Mickey and Joseph, Hopper for once attempts to incorporate elements of conscience and responsibility that his other more notorious characters seriously lack.

Commercial Breakdown

Dennis Hopper in the World of Advertisements

Film actors, directors, and celebrities often make a convenient sideline in advertisements and product endorsements. When a break in the acting schedule allows for an all-expenses-paid excursion, many of them venture afar in pursuit of a big payday for very little work. This facet of celebrity is explored in director Sofia Coppola's film *Lost in Translation* (2003). Bob Harris, played to cynical perfection by Bill Murray, is an ageing Hollywood movie star suffering an existential crisis whilst filming an advertisement campaign for Suntory Whiskey in Tokyo, an engagement that will pay him a handsome two million dollars. Although this film is fictional, the situation is very much based in reality. Sofia Coppola chose Suntory Whiskey for Harris to promote because her father, director Francis Ford Coppola, also endorsed the same drink for the Japanese market in the late 1970s.

The internet is spilling over with bizarre foreign advertisements that were never meant for Western consumption and so fail to sell the idea of the product to a more reserved consumerist market. Television commercials featuring American actors produced for the Japanese market take on a surrealist, madcap vibe. One extreme example is actor Nicolas Cage's extravagant and exuberant commercials for Pachinko, a Japanese arcade game. Cage is well-known for his off-the-wall acting style in a majority of his films, but in these adverts he goes beyond insanity. In a series of Pachinko commercials, Cage sings an improvised song at a grand piano, gets aroused in a cartoonish fashion by the prospect of bedding triplets, and dances on a highway with a legion of alien spacemen. The advertisements add a completely new dimension to Cage's already well-documented extrovert tendencies. Cage is not alone in infiltrating the Japanese market. A whole host of A-list celebrities have left their dignity in the West to make some quick and easy money. Harrison Ford sold Kirin Lager Beer, Sean Connery sold yogurt, Brad Pitt sold jeans, and Paul Newman sold coffee. In 1995, Dennis Hopper himself boarded this particular crazy train. A thirty-second advert promoting a Japanese cleaning product called Tsumura saw Hopper belly deep in a bubble bath playing with a wind-up rubber duck and cackling like a lunatic. However, what looks like indignity and lunacy to us in the West is enthusiastically received in the Asian market and often proves to be a commercial success. Hopper's turn in the Tsumura advertisements saw a huge increase in product sales. According to Tsumura spokesperson

Yukihito Kagawa, "the ad shows a side of him no one knows, and the reaction has been tremendous".[1] I would argue that this side of Hopper, the cackling madman, was actually a side of him for which he was well-known at the time. This being the pinnacle of his antagonist persona, with criminal roles in *Boiling Point, Super Mario Bros, Red Rock West* (all 1993) and *Waterworld* (1995). For Hopper and many other Western celebrities, the decision is clearly a monetary one: as Hopper stated, "I couldn't believe the money they were paying me. If I could do one of these every year, I could retire."[2] But was there any other reason why Hopper chose to frequently appear in advertisements? Hopper saw artistic intent in most media outlets. In some cases the product or the marketing strategy employed reminded audiences of his past achievements and his effect on popular culture. What follows is a study of Hopper's advertisement excursions and an attempt to decipher his reasoning—other than monetary—for appearing in commercials.

To return to the subject of whiskey, Dennis Hopper's first foray into product advertising was to team up with fellow film director John Huston (*Asphalt Jungle, African Queen, Wise Blood*) in a 1972 billboard advertisement for Jim Beam whiskey. The two film icons stand side by side, each raising a tumbler of Jim Beam with ice. The byline reads "Generation gap? Jim Beam never heard of it", whilst a short bio explains the two men's importance. In terms of bridging the gap between old and new, the marketing scheme works. Both directors were critically lauded and cinema audiences lapped up their work, although Huston was the more prolific of the two at the time of the advertisement. However, given that this advert was on the cusp of Hopper's expulsion from Hollywood and his decade-long struggle with drink and drugs, the advert, or at least the use of Hopper, could be seen as being somewhat inappropriate. After the failure of his second film, *The Last Movie*, and his exile from Hollywood, no clear-headed marketing executive would touch Hopper as a drug-taking alcoholic during the 1970s and early 1980s. So Hopper's return to the world of advertisements didn't happen until the late 1980s/early 1990s, when he was clean of drink and drugs and had an air of middle-age respectability about him. As detailed in previous pages, Hopper's return to acting and directing signified a new work ethic that saw him take on nearly any job offered to him, good or bad. Thus, when given the opportunity to appear alongside his younger more rebellious self thanks to the maverick of modern technology, Hopper rose to the occasion.

The television advert for the Ford Cougar from the early 1990s showed that a mainstream—even, one might say, slightly conservative audience—was now fully embracing Dennis Hopper. The commercial shows a middle-aged Hopper cruising the American highways in his brand new Ford Cougar, a highly sensible and very middle-class car. He comes across a lone biker in Death Valley, *Easy Rider*'s Billy, his younger, more irresponsible self. They ride side by side for a short while, they stop and sit together drinking coffee in a diner similar to the one seen in *Easy Rider,* the waitress serving the coffee gives a wink to the older Hopper, whilst simultaneously ignoring his scruffy younger self. They hit the road again until the older Hopper hits the accelerator in his Cougar and leaves Billy behind. Peter Fonda's character Wyatt is notable by his absence.

Hopper's Cougar commercial could be seen as selling out to corporate money and tarnishing his biggest creative success. *Easy Rider's* signature song 'Born to be Wild' by Steppenwolf blasts over the advert, and where once the song characterised freedom and its lyrical imagery reflected perfectly the winding highways that Hopper and Fonda rode, in this commercial's context the song veers into middle-of-the-road, middle-class irony. The fact that 'Born to be Wild' now sits alongside Thin Lizzy's 'The Boys Are Back in Town' and Lynyrd Skynyrd's 'Sweet Home Alabama' as a staple song on CD compilations such as *Born to be Wild* and *Classic Rock* from Time Life Entertainment says something of the song's depleted rebel credentials. 'Born to be Wild' is no longer the anthem for wild youth but instead reflective of a mid-life crisis.

The commercial may cheapen the historical and cultural value of *Easy Rider,* yet the Cougar strategy is effective in reaching out to the target audience of middle-aged, middle-class males who, back in the late 1960s and early 1970s, lived their lives in the shadow of *Easy Rider* and the 1960s counterculture. What Ford's marketing department was hoping was to engage the type of man who holds his youth in a nostalgic haze and is constantly longing to be the carefree individual he once was. With the onset of adulthood and the responsibilities of family and work, the Cougar Man intends to find that inner spark that drove him to once cherish personal freedom and fulfil personal dreams. In a short 'making of' film, the production team behind the commercial classified this as "wild at heart" and noted that "research showed that on the outside, potential Cougar drivers may appear conventional, but hidden on the inside is a younger, wilder spirit. A quality that can be expressed by the car they drive."[3] In this regard, Hopper was perhaps the perfect choice to front the Cougar campaign. After decades under the influence of drugs and drink, Hopper had returned to the fold, a respectable and well-regarded actor with a solid stature of cool. This would appeal to the once rebellious baby boomers who were now (mostly) middle-aged men themselves who had aged alongside Hopper but whose lives no doubt took very different paths into conformity and non-confrontation. The Ford Cougar offers a safe, conservative, family-friendly means of transport with a proposed streak of youthful vigour, designed to quash the all-out rebellion of a mid-life crisis. The short 'making of' documentary shows the painstaking process of stringing together the choreography and synchronisation of the two Hoppers meeting. Regardless of the cheapening effect it may have had on *Easy Rider* at the time, the commercial is a brilliant creative endeavour.

Inevitably, there would come to be some advertisement campaign that would lend itself to Dennis Hopper's late 1980s/early 1990s acting persona of the hyperactive, intense sociopath. The Nike commercials for the National Football League (NFL) allowed Hopper to roll two personalities into one character: Frank Booth's poisoning stare and twitchiness and Howard Payne's wise-cracking mannerisms. Hopper's role as Stanley Cramer, a crazed NFL referee who has clearly hit the skids, was a fixture during the 1994 Super Bowl. With fourteen thirty-second commercials and one minute-and-a-half impassioned monologue, the Nike commercials cost a princely \$3 million and were broadcast to millions of people worldwide, exposing Hopper to one of the largest audiences of his career. Coming hot off the heels of his success in *Speed,* Hopper's role of Stanley Cramer offers a very interesting aspect of his then on-screen persona. In one advert, we find Stanley sitting on a couch looking dishevelled and disorientated, rambling about a football game. There is a scene of him from the past in his clean referee uniform on the pitch, a sign that his life was once better, or perhaps this is a delusion of Stanley's. We learn in a later advert that Stanley never really had a shot at a football career. In the one-minute monologue commercial, Stanley stands in front of a large flag of the Nike Logo much like Sergeant Patton in front of his American flag and delivers a rousing speech that references his past and his love for football:

> When I was a boy, I dreamed of playing football. But I was allergic to milk and the soybean juice substitute that my mother gave me made my bones weak. But I digress. My point is: I love football. Football. The ballet of bulldozers. The moments of grace in a sea of fury. The crowd: fickle, fanatical, and faithful. Every kick-off is a possibility. Every down a war. And every now and then, it doesn't come down to fancy strategy or speed or strength. It comes down to who has more heart. Yes. You see football is in my bones, and where goes the two point conversion, the on-side kick and the TV time-out, so go I. I have seen the locker room my friends. I have smelled the shoes, stormed the field and sung the songs. And I have heard the footsteps. Yes. And they say to me, they say "Stanley, is football the greatest game in the world?" And I say, "Yes, footsteps. Yes it is!"[14]

With its poetic and passionate imagery, the monologue is certainly rousing, and no doubt had the desired result of drumming up the passion of the crowds of football fans before the big game. However, what is interesting about Stanley Cramer is that we know something of his past that possibly leads him to be the strange character that he is. The soybean juice his mother fed him due to his milk allergy instigated his failed dreams of becoming a football player. His weakened bones would not have put him in good stead for a physical sporting career. With this understanding, we see that Stanley is a sad obsessive, possibly an unhinged individual. In comparison to Frank Booth, a certified psychotic, Stanley's sad history is partially explained, whilst Booth's traumatic past is left unspoken. This aspect allows the audience to side with Stanley and even appreciate his obsessive nature.

Over a decade after the Cougar commercial, Hopper matured beyond the idealism of the 1960s, and thoughts turned to retirement. As the baby boomers of the 1960s were retiring alongside him, Hopper seemed a logical choice to front Ameriprise Financial's 'Dreams Don't Retire' investment campaign. Much like the Ford Cougar adverts, Ameriprise's aim was to incorporate a dash of hipness to its otherwise mundane and unhip message and give the generation of Hopper's day another shot at living a free, uncomplicated lifestyle. The marketing research that went into this commercial was meticulous. According to a comprehensive article by Jack Doyle, Ameriprise found its target audience to be a "work hard/play hard cohort who were still rebels in a sense, and were not into passive retirement. Boomers are looking forward to the 'next act' of their lives, but don't want to be lectured about money and financial planning."[5] Hopper was chosen to front the campaign because "Baby Boomers saw Hopper as extremely talented, willing to challenge himself, uncompromising, and just really cool. He is someone they look up to and aspire to emulate his values."[6]

In one of three adverts, Hopper alludes to the 1960s era by proclaiming "Flower power was then, your dreams are now."[7] Another advert draws parallels with the radical politics and cultural shift of the 1960s and attempts to exchange the hopes that many people carried back then with the hope of a carefree retirement today.

> Your dreams are crazy. They're impossible. That's what they said back in the day, when your dreams changed everything. That's not gonna stop now. You're not gonna turn your dreams over to the authorities at age 60. You find someone who believes in your dreams.[8]

Given the context of the target audience and the timing of the advert, Hopper again seemed a well-suited choice to front this campaign. Hopper's appeal lies in his iconic status as a once rebellious young man of the 1960s and 1970s who moved towards conservative values in the late 1980s and 1990s. However, as Bob Garfield points out in his article 'Ameriprise's Dennis Hopper Spot: Wrong Icon, Right Tone', Hopper's casting could cause some cultural confusion, as his previous acting roles have included "a drug smuggler in *Easy Rider*, a brutal pervert in *Blue Velvet*, a sociopathic bomber in *Speed*," and let us not forget an alcoholic child abuser in *Out of the Blue*. In Garfield's opinion, the 1960s generation was not all about "sticking it to the man".[9] Although he represents the 1960s like no other, Hopper's appeal to those of his generation now goes beyond that of 1960s radical. His later persona was one of quiet, maturity, and integrity.

British phone company Orange (now known as EE) executed a well-thought-out and entertaining set of short sketches in its marketing strategy for the company's cinema-related offers. Orange lined up an array of Hollywood stars to help back the promotion in what the company referred to as Gold Spots. Starting in 2003, these short commercials were shown in cinemas as preludes to the main feature film. In the commercials, actors and icons including Steven Seagal, Val Kilmer, Spike Lee, Rob Lowe, and even Darth Vader (voiced by James Earl Jones) would meet with two Orange executives, Mr. Dresden (Brennan Brown) and his associate Mr. Elliot (Steve Furst). Mr. Dresden, "who sees films as an extension of advertising", audaciously apprehends a number of celebrities whilst they're filming and in effect "hijacks their projects with incongruous Orange references."[10] In Orange's world, film is simply a commodity in which to place its product. Dennis Hopper's 2007 Gold Spot sees him pitch his new film idea to Dresden and Elliot. The synopsis involves Hopper playing a stockbroker who loses all his assets and is forced to take the city bus to work. The film is, as Hopper describes it "a collision of cultures". The executives seem interested in Hopper's idea but then begin to adapt Hopper's vision to their own (as they do in all the Gold Spots to serve their need of product placement), asking for a bomb to be planted on the bus and an explosion. One executive asks for Orange's own phone to be used as the device. Hopper is unable to fathom the idea and in a twist on his Howard Payne character from *Speed*, proclaims "No one gets off the bus!" until his idea and his film pitch is seen through.

In 2008, Hopper was commissioned to direct a short 'mini movie' for up-market Italian fashion retailer Tods. His first directorial role since 1994's *Chasers*, Hopper recreated a modern version of the Cinderella story, but instead of a charming prince reacquainting his Cinderella with a lost slipper, the object became a Tods Pashmy bag and the prince a handsome journalist. Set within a bustling Italian market, actress Gwyneth Paltrow meets a dapper journalist for an interview. As the interview begins, paparazzi hound the table and Paltrow runs away, leaving her Tods bag behind. The handsome journalist chases after her eagerly to give her back the bag. The rest of the short film is spent roaming various lively locations as the journalist desperately tries to hand the bag back to Paltrow. Although clearly designed to sell an expensive product, Hopper's film is an artistic attempt at marketing that "is short on dialogue but long on elaborate, richly shot scenes".[11] Hopper himself praised the film, saying "There is a whole Fellini-like ending to the story that is really beautiful."[12]

A number of years before he died, Hopper signed a deal with skateboarding brand Vans. The idea was to produce a clothing line of T-shirts, caps, hooded sweat tops, and trainers adorned with some of Hopper's iconic art and photography. With the clothing range in the later stages of production when Hopper died, it was left to Hopper's eldest daughter Marin to help finish the project. On a bright sunny morning in August 2011, residents of Hopper's former neighbourhood Venice, California were faced with huge posters of the weary face and droopy eyes of *Apocalypse Now*-era Dennis Hopper. Across the middle of the poster was the tagline 'Hopper Lives' in bold white type. Residents fearing the wild man of Hollywood had been resurrected from the dead were calmed by the Vans logo tucked away discreetly in the corner of the billboard. This was not graffiti vandalism or an art installation by one of Venice's many street artists; this was a slick advertisement campaign. What is different about this advertisement campaign was for once Hopper wasn't appealing to a demographic which was instantly familiar with his excessive past or his 1960s persona. Hopper's T-shirt designs and printed sweatshirts held no appeal to the people who saw *Easy Rider* or even *Blue Velvet*. The Vans campaign was an opportunity to draw in a much younger demographic of skateboarders, street artists, snowboarders, BMX bikers, and extreme sports enthusiasts who were unfamiliar with Dennis Hopper's vast output of films and artwork. In many ways, the campaign was only partly successful. A T-shirt featuring a print of Hopper's iconic *Double Standard* photo of the two Standard gas stations is based on a stunning photograph in itself (refer to the essay 'Art and Photography of Dennis Hopper' for a description of this piece), but the photograph is very much a product of its era. It bears no real meaning to modern youth. The nostalgia/retro piece would be lost on the young and hip audience of Vans apparel. However, the photographs of the torn posters upon torn posters that littered the Los Angeles walls in the 1960s work better, as they illicit a street art quality that take on a more modern appeal. In a press release for the collection, Vans stated that: "Dennis Lee Hopper, did, does, and always will represent the iconoclast, the revolution of creative self-expression, the culture of Vans."[13] As strange as it might seem, Vans advertisement campaign works better now that Hopper is no longer with us. If he had been alive whilst the campaign was running, the brand campaign might have fallen short with its young target audience, who may have not been convinced that an aging movie star was really the best person to front a skating brand and line of clothing they could buy into. With the use of the 'Hopper Lives' tagline and the iconography of the black-and-white still image of a druggy Hopper (a point in his life when he shouldn't have been alive), the image becomes timeless.

Hopper's work in advertisements has followed a similar trajectory to that seen in his film and art. He cleverly played on the persona of a 1960s throwback, reinforcing the message of the various campaigns to his own generation's needs and wants. He also drew comparisons with his popular characters in *Easy Rider* and *Speed,* meaning an audience were well prepped for the insanity he showed in such adverts as the NFL and (although not aimed at Western markets) in some respects Tsumura. In the 1998 documentary *The Fine Art of Separating People from Their Money,* director Hermann Vaske explores the advertising industry and its relationship towards art, film, and commerce. Hopper acts as host, introduces the chapters, and explains his passion for adverts and the artistic merits and influential techniques employed in advertising. In the introduction, Hopper asks: "Is it art? Is it business? Should it be shocking? Should it be funny?" In order to determine the meaning of advertisements within popular culture, Vaske interviews film directors who traversed the gap between filmmaking and commercials such as Tony Scott and Alan Parker and gathers together numerous examples of advertising from different countries. Hopper's introductory scenes are insightful, and his knowledge of the mediums explored is vast. Hopper felt that a relationship between commercials and artistic expression certainly existed. Although never completely successful, Dennis Hopper's work in commercials and advertisements did reaffirm his status as an American icon. By cleverly tapping into his various on-screen as well as off-screen personas and alluding to his history within American popular culture, the target audiences of the various campaigns were sold on his iconography.

White Light/White Heat

Actor and Character Collide in *White Star*

The method acting approach, which Dennis Hopper employed throughout his film career, informs the actor that in order to portray the truth on screen, one must believe and immerse oneself within the world and the situations of the character being portrayed. Constantin Stanislavski, the Russian Theatre director, acting coach, and originator of the method, contemplates this in his book *An Actor's Handbook*: "Find out all the reasons which justify the actions for your character and then act without reflecting about just where your 'own' actions end and 'his' begin."[1] The period between *The Last Movie* and *Blue Velvet* saw many examples of Hopper merging his own persona with that of his troubled characters. In some cases it was difficult for the audience (and possibly even for himself) to tell where Hopper's own actions ended and his characters began. *White Star* (1984) directed by Roland Klick is a lucid example of this. When Hopper appeared in *White Star*, he was still in exile from Hollywood, and his health was in serious decline due to the copious amounts of drugs and drink he was ingesting. The music industry in which *White Star* takes place is renowned for its overindulgence in drugs, drink, and hedonism. This was nothing in comparison to the recklessness Hopper had experienced in the last decade and a half. The industry represented in *White Star* is full of degenerate characters, and music manager Kenneth Barlow (Hopper) stands at the centre of it all, a protagonist of organised chaos and perceptive media attention.

White Star came at a transitional phase in Hopper's life and career. When in the process of filming, Hopper was still the outsider from Hollywood. The rebirth of his film career, with films such as *Blue Velvet* and his Oscar-nominated role in *Hoosiers*, was just a few years away. His spiritual rebirth, in which he became clean, was already on the horizon. But at this juncture, *White Star* reveals Hopper in the midst of a serious mental and physical burnout that is horrifically captured in this energetic and utterly chaotic film. It is stated that Hopper "was completely strung out" during the filming process of *White Star* "and could only shoot for a few hours a day between cocaine fixes".[2] Much like the crazy-eyed bushranger in *Mad Dog Morgan,* the hyperactive photojournalist in *Apocalypse Now*, or the welfare-dependent alcoholic father of *Rumble Fish*, Hopper's character Ken Barlow is a reflection of the persona of Dennis Hopper at the time of filming. Hopper is not just on drugs in *White Star*, he *is* the drug in *White Star*. In the run-up to a 2013 screening of the film, New York's Spectacle Theatre described Hopper's appearance as "his most terrifying, unhinged performance".[3] It is easy to understand why, over 25 years later, Dennis Hopper dismissed *White Star*. When asked in an interview by British journalist Piers Morgan what he believed was his worst movie, Hopper stated: "I think one I made in Germany in the early 1980s called *White Star* was the worst, it was absolutely terrible." Hopper then goes on to reveal that it was "Drugs (that) got me through that one".[4] Hopper admitted that despite his dislike of *White Star*, it was "emotionally the most demanding film I've ever made, and therefore the most dangerous one—for me."[5] In the majority of drug and alcohol addictions, the addict's worst moments are rarely, if ever, captured on film in such up-close detail. However, in Hopper's case, there is over a decade of his substance abuse preserved in cinematic, or in some cases, VHS form.

It is fascinating to witness Hopper begin his journey towards what would eventually become his representation of the 1960s burnout. From this point onward, the darkness portrayed on screen in some of Hopper's best performances would reflect the cynicism of the post-1960s years. Barlow is a washed-up music manager whose need to regain respect and notoriety eventually destroys him. This theme emerges in a number of Hopper's later characters—an ensemble of broken souls all somehow shattered by the utopia they experienced in the 1960s, which has since been lost to them. The hippie ex-biker Feck in *River's Edge* recalls his glory days, cruising the highways on his motorcycle, chasing girls; inevitably his experiences turned sour, leaving him lonely and paranoid. Hopper's Mr. Rogers, the spaced-out teacher in the 1980s teen science fiction film *My Science Project*, preps his materialistic students on revolution and the 1960s ideal whilst inhaling gas from a cylinder to gain a quick high. Huey Walker in *Flashback* also holds on to those ideals but ends the film embracing capitalism and its trappings. These characters and many more represent dreams that have been actively snatched away from them or—perhaps more realistically—dreams that have simply faded away as society has moved forwards whilst they continue to look back nostalgically. This post-1960s cynicism was, in effect, already well established in Hopper before the 1960s had even drawn to a close. For example, Billy in *Easy Rider* is by all external appearances a hippie and a radical, but on the inside he is a greedy capitalist, selling out his ideals for a few fast bucks and an easy life. This is one of Hopper's ultimate triumphs in film and art. His association with the 1960s as an iconoclast are well-documented, but his failure to live up to it, the betrayal of those principles, and the damage this betrayal can cause for others (and even himself) is what Hopper ultimately captures on screen.

Set within the punk scene of what looks like a dystopian West Berlin, *White Star* follows the exploits and exploitation of Moody (Terrence Robay), a David Bowie-type new-wave keyboardist and producer who is managed by Kenneth Barlow, a former tour manager for The Rolling Stones. Barlow instigates a number of high-profile marketing stunts for Moody to promote his up-and-coming record *White Star*. These include a debut show in front of a violent mob of Berlin punks that, as foreseen by Barlow, turns into a full-blown riot before Moody gets to play a single note and a disastrous assassination attempt, which turns out to be fatal for a young female fan. Barlow's attempts to shock and awe Moody's fan base and the straight-laced record company executives who are keen to sign Moody operate on the belief that any publicity is good publicity. After a number of near-death experiences, Moody and Barlow part ways. Barlow hits the bottle and then falls to the gutter, while Moody, without his self-destructive manager, signs a contract with the prestigious Eurosounds record label.

We first meet Barlow in a sweaty backstage room at Moody's debut gig. The crowd of punks are getting restless, and Moody paces back and forth nervously in the filthy dressing room, all too aware of the chaos that awaits him on stage. His boyish good looks, crisp white tuxedo, and blonde hair—looking like Luke Skywalker in his white farm boy outfit —are grossly out of place in the sweaty punk-rock environment. Barlow enters the dressing room dressed in a long raincoat and reassures his young protégé. In the space of only a few minutes, we see how volatile Barlow is. The nurturing he demonstrates towards Moody is in violent contrast to his treatment of the club owner, who enters the room and demands that Moody make an appearance on stage. Barlow confronts him up close, spitting and shouting in the club owner's face, until he leaves them in peace. He again reassures Moody and tells him to wait a further five minutes before going onstage. Before leaving the dressing room, Barlow tells Moody to put on a good show, and then menacingly whispers, "Do it man or I'll kill ya." Barlow leaves the dressing room, and Moody is now more nervous than ever before. In the club's corridors, Barlow telephones the police, informing them that a riot is in progress. In fact, the riot has yet to begin. Barlow understands that Moody will not get to play a single note of his electronic soundscapes to the agitated punk mob. When a timid-looking Moody finally arrives onstage, the violent atmosphere has reached boiling point. As Moody's ambient backing track plays, plastic glasses and beer cans hit him repeatedly, and when he finally gets the courage to throw one back, all hell breaks loose. Barlow screams at him to stay onstage and take as much as he can, much like a boxing manager instructing his prizefighter to take the punches being thrown at him. Members of the sound crew try to drag Moody offstage as the crowd smash up anything they can get their hands on. Barlow grabs a bullhorn and screams at the baying mob, "THIS IS THE FUTURE, WHAT DO YOU KNOW ABOUT MUSIC, THIS IS WHITE STAR, THIS IS THE FUTURE." Backstage, Moody has suffered a slashed leg and is somewhat in shock. Barlow insists on leaving the riotous venue through the front door. They emerge onto the Berlin streets, which are now awash with angry punks, uniformed policemen, and the flashing bulbs of the press photographers. As Moody and Barlow climb into a waiting ambulance, Barlow takes a bow and triumphantly proclaims, "Thanks for making me a star, gentlemen." The scene is one of chaos, an exhilarating start for Moody's career and a triumphant marketing success for Barlow. The next day's newspapers and radio shows cover the riot and report that record company Eurosound is interested in offering Moody a record deal.

It is interesting to watch Hopper as Barlow in this opening sequence. There is an uneasiness to his character from the very beginning, a sense of volatility and a genuine fear for the people sharing the screen with him, as if he will "break role, snap their necks, and charge out of the screen at any moment".[6] In fact, it is not how the character is written but rather how Hopper portrays Barlow that makes him so menacing. The volatility of Barlow is all Hopper's own unstable personality being drawn out. These characteristics are fleshed out later in a far calmer but still emotionally fraught scene. Barlow and Moody meet at a night-time café following another chaotic riot in which Moody's recording studio is invaded by Berlin punks who corner a cowering Barlow and proceed to beat him and take turns urinating on him. All this, you have to bear in mind, is orchestrated by Barlow himself. In the aftermath, Barlow and Moody have a brief argument. Barlow takes his urine-stained clothes to the launderette, Moody follows. The scene then plays out loosely with what looks like strong Hopper-led improvisation and reveals a lot more about Barlow's motivation and yearning for success. Barlow slumps down in a corner of the launderette and begins a slurred and rambling account of life in the 1960s during his time with The Rolling Stones. He tells Moody about insane incidents involving Stones guitarist Keith Richards and the band's line-up of sex-crazed groupies. He declares that his generation of rock 'n' rollers were the first real punks, the first generation to rebel against the status quo. He dejectedly admits to Moody that whilst he has not changed, times have, indicating that Barlow is trying to find some kind of meaning in the aftermath of his initial success within a music industry that is now more about marketing strategies than music. In this particular moment, it is hard to distinguish Hopper from Barlow. His admission of "I haven't changed, the times have changed" seems almost like a slip of character, and it is Hopper himself who has come to the realisation that he needs to change. It is also clear in this scene that Barlow feels he has something to prove, as he states: "You know why I wanna do it? Because I wanna show them I can do it again." This is an interesting statement for Barlow to make. Due to the improvisational nature of this scene, it is reasonable to conclude that Hopper is fueling Barlow's own failure in the music industry with his own short-lived success—at this point in time—in the film industry. Of course, during this period there had been many times when Hopper did indeed try once again to prove himself. His directorial return with *Out of the Blue* was uncompromisingly raw in both style and context but was so far removed from the national conscience as to be almost redundant to US audiences. Consider also his turn as the drunken, aloof father in *Rumble Fish* and his unconventional approach to the literary figure Tom Ripley in *The American Friend*. All these performances showed Hopper to be a highly versatile actor and director. However, mainstream Hollywood and audiences alike ignored this. *White Star* is a phenomenal example of the collision between actor and character. The dualities of film and reality coming together to create a personal testimony for the audience. This may not have been the film's—or even Hopper's—original intention, but it is difficult not to interpret what is happening on screen in this way, especially within the broader context of Hopper's personal and professional life.

One of the most heartbreaking performances of Hopper's entire career is nestled within the last ten minutes of *White Star*. Although we have already seen multiple examples of Barlow's destructive nature and troubled mind, it is in these last few moments that Barlow falls apart. After the planned assassination attempt on Moody leaves a young fan dead, Moody begins to realise that the marketing schemes of his manager are ruining him and his chance for a career in music. Barlow agrees with him and they part ways. Barlow drives his Mercedes through the rain-lashed streets of West Berlin whilst supping on a bottle. The world outside his car is unfamiliar and menacing to him. He babbles at himself, asking "Where am I going, where am I going?" He breaks down—crying one second, regaining his composure the next, and then bursting into tears again. He smiles and waves to passers-by, looking perhaps for some recognition or familiarity, but he gets none in return. His frustration increases with the outside world. He berates the driver of a passing car, snarls insults to no one. It makes for uncomfortable viewing; the moment lasts close to five minutes and is one long darkened shot of a destroyed man. He pulls up beside a train station entrance and slumps on the stairs, still slugging from the bottle. Barlow crashes to the floor and with tear-stained eyes looks up at the dispersing clouds, which reveal the glimmering white stars. There is a real sense of free-form performance that litters this scene, but the loose style compliments and perfectly captures the end of the journey that both Barlow and Hopper were on. It is particularly heartbreaking to watch, knowing that in the context of his later career, Hopper would never give such an openly personalised, raw, and visceral performance as this again. However, continuing in this vein would have destroyed Hopper long before he reached his pinnacle comeback year of 1986, and those particular roles would have been completely unobtainable for him in the state of mind he had reached in *White Star*.

Dennis Hopper's *Apocalypse Now* co-star Marlon Brando learnt a similar lesson during the making of the sexually explicit *Last Tango in Paris* (1972). Like *White Star*, it shows an actor reaching into a very personal place to portray the emotional essence on screen (employing method). The film's director Bernardo Bertolucci, wanted to show the sexual and emotional damage of the two characters, which he achieved at the expense of Brando and his co-star Maria Schneider's sanity. Schneider would go on to say that she felt "raped and humiliated"[7] by both Brando and Bertolucci and that the film was one of her biggest regrets. Brando would later state that he would never make another movie like that and refused to speak to Bertolucci for fifteen years after the film was released. Brando was true to his word. He would never again make such an openly explicit and raw film. In fact, after *Last Tango in Paris*, Brando turned up mostly as a cameo performer, adding weight (often physical) to films such as *Superman* (1978) and *The Score* (2001), and was even nominated for a Golden Raspberry Award for Worst Supporting Actor in *The Formula* (1980). Perhaps Dennis Hopper felt that once he had gotten himself clean and sober, he had given enough of himself over to his art. However, unlike Brando, Hopper had no one to blame but himself, for it is Hopper who openly exposes himself and not director Roland Klick who encourages him.

In *White Star*, we have a less blurry snapshot, more a full frontal, of what Hopper was emotionally working through during his wilderness years, and it is an incredibly savage portrait. Barlow is one of many roles, which blurred the line between character and actor in turmoil; starting with the photojournalist in *Apocalypse Now*, moving to Don Barnes in *Out of the Blue*, and ending with Barlow in *White Star*. After this point, even his most menacing and chaotic characters—Frank Booth included—would be tainted with a cartoonish absurdity.

Double Standards

The Art and Photography of Dennis Hopper

Dennis Hopper's last film appearance was in Belgian artist Nicolas Provost's 22-minute short film *Stardust* (2010). The film featured Las Vegas cityscapes, busy street scenes, members of the public, and also celebrities being filmed unawares using a high-resolution digital camera. Provost then edited the footage to create a narrative using the language of Hollywood films. Provost recorded Hopper innocently talking in a McDonald's restaurant with fellow actor Danny Trejo. Their unheard dialogue is replaced with cliché gangster talk. Provost also captured Jack Nicholson leering at some girls as they pass him by in a Las Vegas night club. It is fitting that Hopper's last appearance on film would be in an artistic context. Running parallel to his decade-long regression in mainstream film and reliance on straight-to-DVD movies, Hopper faced a resurgence of interest in his artwork and photography. It is a fascinating paradox, in that Hopper's artistic expression in photography, painting, and sculpture is acknowledged as uncompromisingly passionate and raw, yet a majority of his film work in the last decade of his life would appear, at least at face value, to be the complete opposite.

An exhibition of his collected artwork entitled *Dennis Hopper and the New Hollywood* that went on display at The Cinémathèque Française in Paris collected together photographs, sculptures, found pieces, and screenings of his more revered film work. The exhibition moved on to the Australian Centre for the Moving Image in Melbourne. A coffee table book of the same name highlighting Hopper's own artwork, art collection, interviews, and musings on art and film was produced in conjunction with the exhibitions. Throughout the last decade, monographs of Hopper's photographic work and art pieces were also published to coincide with numerous exhibitions throughout the world. After his death in 2010, extensive and expensive tomes of his photography were published, most notably *Dennis Hopper: Photographs 1961-1967* (Taschen 2009) and *Dennis Hopper: The Lost Album* (Prestal 2012), which coincided with a touring exhibition of photos and prints found tucked away in a drawer after Hopper's death. The more recently released monograph *Dennis Hopper: Drugstore Camera* (Damiani 2015) was a collection of improvised shots using cheap store-bought instamatic cameras that clearly illustrated Hopper's eye for candid photography. Hopper's new found esteem within the art world reached its culmination in

2007 when he presented the British Turner Prize to artist Mark Wallinger for his exhibition *State Britain*.

Hopper was first introduced to contemporary art by frequenting up-and-coming art galleries and studios of Los Angeles and New York in the late 1950s and early 1960s. At the time, Hopper was just soaking up the creativity around him, taking photographs of the artists and gallery shows with his trusty "Nikon camera with 28mm lens exclusively with Tri-x film, which allowed for flexibility and immediacy,"[1] two staple functions of Hopper's photography. He was also producing art alongside his acting career. Hopper took his inspiration from everywhere: he observed art in everything and soaked up influence and inspiration. His work covered almost every movement and genre, from abstract painting, pop art, installation and found pieces to sculpture. As with his film work, where Hopper would adapt his own style and manner to suit the type of film or character, in art he also modified his approach to create a personalised concept of any given artistic genre. Interestingly, as we shall see, Hopper's artwork reflected his personal circumstances, and whilst his life was in turmoil, his work would reflect this, becoming much darker, angrier, and disturbing.

As an audience, we perceive Dennis Hopper's film and artwork as two separate entities. For us, the line that divides film and canvas never blurs. Even his directorial work in *Easy Rider* and *The Last Movie* can be viewed as having artistic intent, but as a whole, a cinema-going audience will always observe it as a movie, a form of media designed to entertain, not necessarily to educate or inform us. This is not how Hopper or others, such as Dutch art historian Rudi Fuchs, perceived his art or film work. Fuchs suggests that Hopper's acting and directing "activities are inextricably linked with that same artistry at the actual center of his existence".[2] Hopper's films are an expression of art, and he saw the mediums of art and film as being able to achieve the same thing. Film directing or film acting in Hopper's mind was equal to painting, taking photographs, or creating sculpture. Even collecting artwork was something that he saw as a creative function, a way in which the piece would continue to thrive and redefine itself under his brief ownership. In a short documentary produced by EarDog Productions, in which Hopper guides the filmmakers around his LA home and studio space, he explains his theory:

> At best, what you can do with collecting is to make sure you take care of the pieces, because you are really just a custodian of them, and hopefully they will live on beyond your lifetime.[3]

He also goes on to explain his philosophy towards collecting as "not buying bankable names, but buying people who I believe are contributing something to my artistic life."[4] The young Dennis Hooper was as an empty vessel, his influences from film, art, and literature filling him until his own creativity spilled out. Repeatedly he would need to ingest every aspect of this creativity that he surrounded himself with in order to continue creating something. He considered it his lifeblood. Much like his influences in acting and directing, Hopper took inspiration for his own art from the many forms of art he saw as a gallery bum in the early 1960s. This need to explore all artistic aspects gave Hopper a desire to create himself. As he explains in the EarDog documentary:

> As an actor I read a book called *Six Lessons in Acting* by Richard Boleslavsky, and in it he says "have you read the great literature, have you seen the great paintings, do you know the great sculptures, do you know the music of your day" so I went off to find paintings cause I thought it would enhance my life as an actor.[5]

Hopper's involvement with the emerging art gallery scene in Los Angeles and his friendships with the new and exciting artists of the day such as Andy Warhol, Marcel Duchamp, and in particular the numerous contributing artists of the LA Ferus Gallery saw Hopper inundated with influences when it came to creating himself.

Writer Howard Hampton best describes Dennis Hopper's photographic works as an "unfolding narrative of the 1960s at the intersection of Pop Art and Hollywood" and as "virtual stills from the greatest unmade film of the 1960s".[6] Dennis Hopper's art and photography evolved along with his acting and directing career, moving and commenting on the times and veering into experimental techniques as and when the technology allowed. His photography work from the 1960s is a document of the era, an exposé of the lives of American people living in a turbulent yet also hopeful decade. Illustrating a vibrant "America, its creativity burgeoning in the arts, liberating itself from the confinement and censorship of the 1950s—the youth revolt",[7] Hopper documented youth with photos of his fresh-faced New Hollywood clique. His work takes in the glitz and glamour of the people who populated the movement with improvisational portraits of his contemporaries in film and art: Paul Newman, Dean Stockwell, and Jane Fonda as well as his artistic acquaintances Andy Warhol, Roy Lichtenstein, and David Hockney. But Hopper's candid black-and-white photography "seemingly stripped them of their glamorous aura, presenting as real folks living their real lives. The photographs look spontaneous and intimate, capturing the subjects off guard or in close-ups."[8] He also took photos of the musicians and bands important to the decade's cultural upheaval: The Byrds, Brain Jones from The Rolling Stones, Ike and Tina Turner. Hopper documented revolt in the civil rights marches that brought a new era of political participation by marginalised groups. For example, his photographs of Martin Luther King Jr. addressing an audience of civil rights marchers in 1963 has become an iconic image of the movement. Talking into a tangle of microphones, King appears to be sidelined into the edge of the frame. Hopper's intention of centering the microphones within the frame of the picture could be signifying that the message delivered is more important than the person delivering the words. The ideals and expectations of those King addressed were a shared concern. King fluently communicated these ideals to the people, but the movement began before Martin Luther King Jr. and continued to gain momentum after his death.

Much like his fast and vibrant directorial work, the photographs—though predominantly black and white in this medium—capture movement, emotion, expression, and an essence that something important is happening unseen and outside of the frame. Hopper was always attempting to make social comments. Considering the social and political content of his work, it should come as no surprise that Hopper documented one of the most seismic events in recent American history: the assassination of John F. Kennedy. The piece entitled *Kennedy Funeral on Television* (1963) shows eight grainy still frame close-up shots from the state procession of President Kennedy that was televised to the nation. The piece conjures up the grief of the national conscience, yet it also points towards hope and courage in the face of despair, an act of bringing a nation together under the banner of loss and anguish. In frames six and eight, when the American flag is draped over the coffin that carries the dead president, this instantly evokes pride and audacity within the viewer and reminds us that a hero to the American people lies under the flag, potentially a martyr for the American Dream. However, a certain distance is suggested within the piece. By witnessing the event on television (as many would have done), Hopper is perhaps commenting on the detachment and coldness of television and modern culture. The first photo shows the television at a distance. Kennedy's iconic image, taken from archival footage of when he was alive, lights up on screen. In the next shot, we are up close to the television screen, as if the funeral was just something that happened to be on or something stumbled upon whilst aimlessly flicking channels in a motel room. Hopper also used the same technique of photographing images from the televised moon landing, again a national event witnessed by many via television and which Hopper commented upon as "when a president of ours was assassinated and we went to the moon because of him".[9]

As mentioned above, Hopper's documenting of the Civil Rights Movement gave an important and honest portrayal of the hopes and dreams of a socially underprivileged part of the American population. One piece entitled *Selma, Alabama* (*Full Employment*) (1965) illustrates the determination of the young Black-American community to gain equal rights and opportunities in the future of America. The young man who stands centre frame shoots the camera a glare of determination and a belief in what he wishes to achieve for himself and others. Behind the young man, a young woman casually hoists an American flag over her shoulder, a symbol of patriotism, belief, and pride in a country that still had a lot to achieve in terms of equality and fairness. Hopper's own view of his photography from this period suggests that he believed the images he was taking were significant: "I wanted to document something. I wanted to leave something that I thought would be a record of it, whether it was Martin Luther King, the hippies, or whether it was the artist".[10]

Double Standard (1964) is one Hopper's more famous photographic works. Described in some detail in a previous essay, the photograph "captures an image of the American road that is both historically fraught and formally complex."[11] *Double Standard* emerges as an unsentimental comment on post-war American society. Situated in the middle of the frame is a Standard Oil gas station with two signs side by side reading 'Standard'. A billboard above the station reads, "Smart Women cook with gas in balanced power homes", a materialistic advertisement aimed at the domesticated woman of America. This image was prior to the full escalation of American involvement in the Vietnam War and a time when people still believed the war was a reasonably just cause. America was excelling in terms of business, capitalism, and materialism, and socially the country was addressing the issue of civil rights with the passing of the Civil Rights Act of 1964. A sense of optimism prevailed, which can be witnessed in *Double Standard*. The photo is framed by a cemented road and a dark foreboding sky that almost matches in colour, lighting up the scene ahead, framing the image within. In the rear-view mirror we see a line of cars, which on closer inspection appear to have no drivers at the wheel. There is an absence of people in the shot, although they are present in terms of being there (in cars, inside the gas station) apart from a sole figure who stands alone on the sidewalk in between the two roads, looking like he's waiting for someone or is just lost. It is an exceptional, seemingly impromptu photograph that conjures up a defining image of early 1960s America. It is also, in retrospect, recognisably a Dennis Hopper photograph. With an added dash of colour, it resembles the last few moments of *Easy Rider* in which Billy and Wyatt ramble through an industrialised landscape, the first time in the film that we see a truly modern environment. However, what is most apparent in this photo are the two roads heading off in opposite directions and into an unknown distance, two very different directions to be taken. In his own career, Hopper also walked two very different roads. One is the creative, passionate and independent artist, the person responsible for creating such work as *Double Standard, Easy Rider, The Last Movie*, and *Out of the Blue*—works that distil the integrity of the artist. The other road Hopper took led to compromise and to movies such as *Super Mario Bros.* With a few exceptions, a distinct lack of integrity was persistent in the last decade of his film career. With the onset of his directorial career in 1969, Hopper abandoned photography for the next twenty years. For us the audience, this represents a huge gap in his artistic life, and an unfortunate lack, at least for the spectator, of documentation for the spiralling madness that would befall him (and America) from the 1970s to mid-1980s. When he finally returned to the medium in the late 1980s, his principles, approach, and technique had changed, and so had the technology. In the 1960s, Hopper had documented his surroundings, the people, the changing landscape of popular culture, and public life in spontaneous bold black-and-white photographic film. His new method seemed to drop the social and political commentary and focused more on the personal. A self-portrait from 1997 entitled *Within a man of light, there is only light, within a man of darkness, there is only darkness* shows two dark images of Hopper silhouetted against a bright white background. In the first portrait, the interior of Hopper's silhouette is a bright lens flare that emerges from the head and trails down the front of the figure. In the second portrait, the interior of the figure is completely black. This is a compelling work of experimental photography, and given Hopper's own personal history, it could be argued to be a comment on his own past and internal demons. The 'man of light', which we assume is the clean, sober, and sane Hopper, attracts the eye of the observer, whilst the 'man of darkness' lingers to the side, evoking a sinister presence or an echo of a darker interior self or past. Although Hopper had survived a great deal of personal trauma, he had come out the other side stronger and more determined. What Hopper appears to be letting the spectator understand is that even though he recovered, darkness and a sense of guilt still lingers.

Whereas in the 1960s Hopper would use his camera as a tool to capture a spontaneous moment, his later photographic works rely on set-up and composition. Comparing his spur-of-the-moment photograph of 1960s stars Andy Warhol, James Brown, and Jane Fonda with his 2006 portraits of Robert Downey Jr, Michael Madsen, Charlie Sheen, and Jon Voight, there is an impression of composure from the subjects, the knowledge that they are having their picture taken. After a twenty-year hiatus, Hopper's use of this medium perhaps became something more akin to a leisure pursuit. This certainly seems likely in his decision to photograph a porn shoot for the American pornographic magazine *Hustler* in the late 1980s for a series called 'Celebrity Porn'.

During the production of the straight-to-DVD noir thriller *Out of Season* (2004), Hopper used the unique shooting location of Romania to experiment in digital photography. The outcome of this was the slim monograph *Bucharest Nights* (Percival Press, 2005), which was described by art blogger Patrick Harris as "ghostly and ethereal. Stark figures in golden tones against a black backdrop, light trails down a street, neon glows from a casino."[12] The photographs collected in *Bucharest Nights* still capture spontaneity, but the focus here is on experiment and even voyeurism. Jan Hein Sassen observes that Dennis Hopper's "art continues to deal with the problematics of reality versus illusion, photography versus painting".[13] A truer statement could not be said regarding Hopper. The theme of reality and illusion has become a staple of Hopper's work, not only in art but also in film. *The Last Movie*, for example, is a testament to what we perceive as a reality or an illusion. The act of filmmaking is a creation of illusion and spectacle, and Hopper playfully confuses the audience into what they should comprehend. In his artwork, Hopper mixed mediums in a chaotic fashion, a fusion of styles and abstract forms often gathering in one piece. Hopper's earliest pieces resemble the abstract expressionism that was infiltrating the more traditional art scene of the time. Sassen comments that for Hopper, abstract expression had "a natural appeal for him, however, it was anti-illusionist, painting for the sake of painting."[14] Unfortunately, most of Hopper's earliest pieces were lost when a fire ripped through his Los Angeles home, destroying most of his work. Only one piece survives from that time, an untitled abstract oil painting, which was at the time on display in an LA gallery. Although a brilliantly textured piece, it is clear that Hopper was experimenting with form and would go on to produce more daring work in the years ahead.

The Pop Art movement, the mixed media collage, as well as the found piece heavily influenced Hopper's artwork in the early to mid-1960s. Two examples of the found piece are his *Mobil Man* and *Salsa Man*. Originally used as roadside advertisements for a Mobil garage and a Spanish Mexican restaurant, the 26-foot-tall fibreglass statues have been taken out of their original context to become something more profound: a comment on consumerism and an overindulgent advertising culture. Another found piece which echoes Andy Warhol's own pop art work is *Coca Cola Sign* (1961), a tin sign used possibly as a store window display, with four cola bottles and thermometers showing the suggested serving temperature. It is interesting to see that Hopper seems to find his found art in product advertising. It could be argued that this was Hopper's intention with these found pieces, a comment on puerile marketing tactics that were being used by every industry in America at the time, including the film industry that Hopper was working within. In 1963, Hopper collaborated with his artistic mentor Marcel Duchamp (the influential artist who produced the found piece *Fountain*, a men's urinal taken out of the bathroom and placed in a gallery setting) on the found piece *Hotel Green* (*Entrance*), a door sign to a hotel entrance that points guest towards the entrance. The hand pointing towards the right perhaps illustrates Duchamp's theory that "the artist of the future will merely point his finger and say it's art—and it will be art."[15] Hopper in this case takes the finger-pointing literally.

Hopper entered something of a dry spell during the 1970s; the disappointment with being shunned from Hollywood a second time after *The Last Movie* and his drink and drug misuse kept him somewhat preoccupied. He did famously collaborate with Andy Warhol on one of his Chairman Mao pieces, although the collaboration was prompted by an act of paranoia and violence as opposed to an artistic endeavour. The screen-print image of Chinese communist leader, Chairman Mao, with Warhol's distinctive high contrast colouring, was shot at twice by a spooked, and one might assume, intoxicated Hopper in 1972. Warhol circled the bullet holes and labelled them "Warning Shot" to the bullet that hit just above Mao's shoulder and "Bullet Hole" for the shot that hit the eye, and proclaimed the piece an artistic collaboration between the two of them. By the end of the 1970s and early 1980s, Hopper's excessive drug and drink use had reached a critical point. Unable to command a reputable career in film, his roles were mostly embodiments of his own outrageous persona (*White Star, Mad Dog Morgan*). This craziness was caught on camera during a career retrospective at the Rice Media Centre in Houston, Texas, in 1984. An inebriated Hopper readies the audience for what will be an art happening, a death-defying stunt called The Russian Suicide Chair. Spectators were bussed to a nearby speedway and watched with bated breath as Hopper surrounded himself with live dynamite and simultaneously ignited the sticks to create a vortex that shielded him from the explosion. One misplaced stick would have blown him to pieces. This moment was in turn an artistic resurrection (possibly triggered by the near-death experience). After a decade of producing little to no artistic works, Hopper began experimenting with paint again. The untitled works produced between 1982/1983 are considered "abstract expressionist and collage-like, as though he needs to start from the very beginning".[16] There is certainly evidence of Hopper attempting to rekindle his artistic spark with these pieces, and Rudi Fuchs observes that "the artist was in a hurry. Once more, after all those years, he wanted to put into practice all that he still knew from the old days: the movements of the hand and the controlling keenness of the eye."[17] The works are darker in tone and expel many of the pop art influences in order to concentrate on the expressionist. In terms of Hopper's state of mind, the abstracts speak volumes. An acrylic entitled *X-Xerox* (1982) exposes a statement of depression, like a spiralling and cracking film reel. The paintings produced in 1982-1983 show a private expression of creativity, a testing of the waters, and a regaining of confidence in the field. When his film comeback occurred in 1986, Hopper's state of mind and his artwork was revived with a sense of positivity and freedom. The *Morocco* series of paintings, which date from 1994, are bold and colourful. Reds, oranges, and blues with dashes of white and black reflect a very different mood from anything Hopper had produced previously. The paintings have "an earthy brown overtone upon which a loose pattern of forms is painted in different colors."[18] They suitably reflect Hopper's ease with a paintbrush. The works appear effortless with composure and full of life. In comparison, the series of works produced later entitled *Florence* (1996) and *Amsterdam* (1998-1999) are more subdued and pale and seem less vital. Nevertheless, these works still show Hopper to be an inspired artist, working within a medium he clearly felt comfortable with.

In Hopper's earlier directorial film work, he was often perceived as uncompromising. The looseness and even the content of *Easy Rider* was at odds with the current film market of the time, whilst *The Last Movie* was so far removed from the mainstream that it was barely understood by critics and audiences as a narrative piece. *Out of the Blue* was as disturbing and nihilistic as any of the post-punk films of the early 1980s. *Colors* mostly towed the mainstream line, but the film's downbeat tone, drug referencing, and violent gang warfare meant that the film maintained a strong critical voice, again at odds with mainstream cinema at the time. When compromise began to occur in his later film work, he withdrew his name from the product, as witnessed by his film *Catchfire*. Hopper attempted to bridge the gap between mainstream film and his dedication to art and artists by incorporating artistic elements within the movies he directed. On some level, they were mostly successful, certainly visually, as witnessed in *Easy Rider* and *The Last Movie's* raucous editing techniques influenced by European art house.

Hopper produced impressive art, photographs, and sculptures, and for this, he is effectively faultless and universally recognised in artistic circles for his uncompromising output. However, his film work is a different matter altogether. The faults appear on a regular basis, especially as his career progressed—or dwindled—into the 2000s. What Hopper's film work shows is that unlike other art forms, film can be considered abysmal and still find a small but somewhat appreciative audience. One example is the film *The Room* (2003), directed by Tommy Wiseau, which despite being so terrible in acting, dialogue, and direction has still garnered an obsessive cult following. Bad photographs, bad art, and bad sculpture are seldom tolerated in serious art circles; they simply become novelty or are reduced to ridicule. Of course, art is down to personal preference and interpretation. When a spectator observes a form or art, they garner pleasure and appreciation from it. The audience recognises it as being a superior, important piece of art or, depending on our interpretation, we reject it altogether. This is not the case with film. An audience can view a bad film and still find redeeming qualities or, most often, some moments of hilarity—again, *The Room* is a perfect example. This is something that rarely happens in other artistic mediums. It is certainly something that Dennis Hopper never chose to explore in his works of art and photography. Dennis Hopper made great art, but he did not always make great movies. It is a shame that the aspect of Dennis Hopper's career that he is most known for is often where he is least appreciated. His artistic works have rarely, if ever, received the same critical mauling, or praise, that his film work has.

Coda

The Fourth Wall

There is a scene nestled within Dennis Hopper's *Easy Rider* that, at first glance, offers a relatively comedic moment in an otherwise serious film. However, upon further analysis, this scene momentarily destabilises the narrative of *Easy Rider*, allowing for a brief reflection from the audience. The scene goes as follows: Billy and Wyatt sit around a campfire smoking a real joint of marijuana whilst hillbilly lawyer George Hanson, a little stoned himself after his first inhale of marijuana, explains to them the conspiracy theory that the extraterrestrial Venusian race is infiltrating human society. George boldly states: "they are people just like us, except that their society is more highly evolved. I mean, they don't have no wars, they've got no monetary system, they don't have any leaders." When this theory is called into question by Hopper's character Billy, George continues: "The Venusians have contacted people in all walks of life…all walks of life…" George (or now as the character is broken, Jack Nicholson) then momentarily breaks into hysterics. The scene cuts to Billy and Wyatt's reaction as George regains his composure. Although the scene feels heavily improvised, according to the film's cinematographer Laszlo Kovacs: "…Jack was in control. He was *so* stoned, but he was so great. He remembered every word."[1] Nicholson's crack-up was kept in the film, possibly to emphasize the corrupting power of drugs on the relatively straight-laced Hanson. However, it briefly throws the audience out of the narrative loop, breaking the imaginary fourth wall that separates actor from spectator in cinema and theatre. Nicholson's character does not address the audience directly, but for a moment the facade of George Hanson drops and Nicholson is revealed. This small but memorable moment begins a career-long practice by Dennis Hopper in breaking down, or in some respects acknowledging, a fourth wall in cinema, yet also an acknowledgement of the fourth wall in the persona of Dennis Hopper.

In an essay entitled "The *Easy Rider* Paradox", published in *Empty Mirror* and included in the book *U.ESS.AY: Politics and Humanity in American Film*, I argue that throughout his post-*Easy Rider* career, Dennis Hopper continually and audaciously referenced his most popular and culturally significant film whilst appearing in or directing other films. To summarise the argument, Hopper would often throw song lyrics from the *Easy Rider* soundtrack into other films, as he did in *The American Friend* when his character Tom Ripley begins bellowing 'The Ballad of Easy Rider' as he looks out towards the Berlin skyline. On the other hand, and far more blatantly, he would appear as an apparition of his *Easy Rider* character, Billy, as witnessed in *My Science Project* (as the stoned teacher Mr. Roberts) and most evidently in *Flashback* (as 1960s activist Huey Walker). As previously discussed, after escaping from the law, Huey Walker sits in a bar and proclaims that "It takes more than going down to your local video store and renting *Easy Rider* to be a rebel". This creates a vortex within the film that sucks the audience from the fiction of *Flashback* into reality. This destabilising trend that Hopper employs is not just unique to *Easy Rider* but is evident in his whole life and career. Hopper's self-referencing of his own cultural credence and intentional breaking of the imaginary fourth wall on a number of occasions dislodges the audience from their perception of viewing a fictional narrative.

A certain dialectical use of words or phrases would also reflect back on Hopper's 1960s persona. One in particular stands out. The continuous use of the term 'man' throughout his entire career offers an admittedly minuscule pathway back to the character of Billy in *Easy Rider.* The hyperactive photojournalist in *Apocalypse Now* passionately rants in regards to Colonel Kurtz: "Are they going to say he was a kind man? He was a wise man? He had plans? He had wisdom? Bullshit, man!" And over twenty-five years later in *Land of the Dead*, Hopper's character Paul Kaufman proclaims "Zombies, man. They creep me out." This continued use of an outdated term offers the audience a preconceived back-story to the characters—which also matches up with Hopper's own past—that somehow, somewhere along the line they were 1960s radicals.

In his second directorial film, *The Last Movie*, Hopper commented ruthlessly on the movie business and its effects on the indigenous people, who see some sort of magic in the fakery of filmmaking. Throughout the movie, we see the inhabitants of the small village set up a mock film set with bamboo stick cameras and flammable torches to simulate lighting rigs. Hopper's character in the movie, stuntman Kansas, reluctantly becomes the film's star, and his death scene is 'filmed' in dramatic slow motion as he is gunned down repeatedly from different angles. As the audience perspective settles on what we believe to be a dead man, we have at this point no reason to believe that the film we are watching is a fake, and yet Kansas gets up from the floor, dusts himself down, and walks off screen. He is not dead, he was acting, and the whole film becomes a ruse. As the death scene is repeated from different angles, Kansas again falls on the dusty ground, but this time he rolls over and sticks his tongue out directly to the camera and towards the audience watching. Hopper has fooled us into thinking that we were watching a real movie narrative, when in fact it was a fake narrative. This is perhaps the most brilliant aspect of *The Last Movie*. It is understandable why the film caused such a critical backlash at the time. Audiences and critics alike were unprepared to have the illusion of the movies broken.

A decade later, Hopper would get the opportunity to direct *Out of the Blue*, a very disturbing film about the corruption of a young girl. He adapted his technique to a film that required a very short production shoot and edit timeframe, producing a seething critique of post-1960s America. The film often makes for uncomfortable viewing, yet tucked away within its narrative is a short scene that breaks through the film's darkness and reminds the audience that what we are watching is not factual. The young protagonist Ceebee runs away from her dysfunctional family life to the city, where she wanders the streets and attends a punk rock concert. One scene from her excursion to the city has her walking down a busy street alongside a man with a music player and a very tight-fitting Elvis Presley-style jumpsuit, singing a haphazard version of Presley's 'Are You Lonesome Tonight?'. Ceebee passes the camera along with her musical companion, and they wander a few more feet down the avenue with their backs to the camera (Ceebee's denim jacket features an emblazed Elvis). The Music Man then stops and turns directly towards the camera, Ceebee turns with him, facing the camera, she then begins clapping, as does the film crew behind the camera. A very distinct cheer comes from Dennis Hopper himself, who in this context is playing the abusive and drunken father to Ceebee. The Music Man walks directly up to the camera and asks if his take was good. It is an audacious moment that takes the audience out of the film and into a moment of reality.

Dennis Hopper's film and artistic career is strewn with remnants of past characters and also characteristics from Hopper himself. As the 1980s began to propel Hopper toward a comeback, he seemed to want to remind audiences of his own perceived persona of the 1960s radical. The character of Huey Walker is an accumulation of this. But before Walker, Hopper appeared briefly in Robert Altman's unsuccessful teen comedy *O.C. and Stiggs* (1985) as the character Sponson, a Vietnam-obsessed paranoiac. Sponson intentionally resembles the photojournalist from *Apocalypse Now*: he wears a camera around his neck, wears the same army-issue camouflage T-shirt and combats, and is even introduced by The Doors' hypnotic song 'The End', a signature song of *Apocalypse Now's* soundtrack. That same year, Hopper gave a wacky performance in teen science fiction film *My Science Project* in which he played teacher Mr. Roberts, an anti-authoritarian throwback to the 1960s. When Mr. Roberts is transported back to that era via an alien technology, he experiences his youth once again and returns to the 1980s in full hippie attire. Mr. Roberts emerges, we assume, as Billy from *Easy Rider*. Even in one of Hopper's last performances, *Swing Vote*, his past comes back to haunt him in a blink-and-you'll-miss-it scene in which demonstrators protest Donald Greenleaf's presidential candidacy. The placards the protesters hold up feature an infamous 1975 mug shot of Hopper, looking worse for wear with tired eyes and shaggy hair, taken when he was arrested for reckless driving.

It must be noted how this phenomenon is almost completely unique to Hopper. No other actor of his generation has continuously attempted to bandwagon so blatantly their past endeavours and iconography. Although Robert De Niro did parade his infamous line "Are you looking at me?" from *Taxi Driver* (1976) when he appeared as Fearless Leader in the kids' film *Adventures of Rocky and Bullwinkle* (2000), this hardly counts as cultural regurgitation on De Niro's part. Marlon Brando came the closest to caricature by portraying a virtually identical version of his iconic Vito Corleone role from *The Godfather* (1972) in the comedy *The Freshman* (1990), in which he plays gangster Carmine Sabatini. The comparison is so blatant that the film even references the similarity by suggesting the Corleone character was based on Sabatini, even though the same actor plays both roles. Only Arnold Schwarzenegger has parodied so closely his past roles, most notably his take on the fearsome cyborg from *The Terminator* (1984), whose infamous line "I'll be back" has cropped up countless times in Schwarzenegger's subsequent films. The catchphrase even crossed over to reality during Schwarzenegger's term as governor of California in his many public addresses.

When Hopper hosted *Saturday Night Live* in May 1987, he appeared as Frank Booth in a game show skit called *What's That Smell?* in which contestants had to inhale through a gasmask and correctly identify the aroma. Despite playing it for laughs and not being able to swear in the manner of Frank Booth (having to use the word "freak" instead of "fuck"), Hopper's performance turns sinister when he inhales from his own gas cylinder and begins frantically screaming at the contestants. This instantly transports the maniacal rapist of *Blue Velvet* into reality. As previously discussed, Hopper's post-*Blue Velvet* career carried with it a trace of Frank Booth throughout. However, if we believe the words Hopper spoke to director David Lynch when taking on the role, "I must play Frank because I am Frank",[2] then we can only assume that remnants of Hopper also exist within all the post-*Blue Velvet* characters he portrayed. The fourth wall is broken repeatedly, simply by Hopper's proximity to the characters. In addition, let us not neglect the rather obvious fact that Dennis Hopper was no on-screen chameleon. In character, Dennis Hopper looked, acted, glared, laughed, smiled, and spoke like Dennis Hopper (he was never one for applying accents). Indeed, he broke the fourth wall by simply being himself. The characters he portrayed were entombed within a well-established individualistic nature, and these characters had to literally scream and shout their way out.

In his book *Breaking the Fourth Wall: Direct Address in the Cinema*, Tom Bloom identifies various forms of direct address throughout the history of cinema. Although Hopper rarely spoke or acknowledged the audience directly within his films (*The Last Movie* certainly, and perhaps to a lesser extent the last scene of *The River's Edge*), his own persona and history broke through this imaginary fourth wall. Using Bloom's analyses, I believe Hopper occupied a "superior epistemic position within the fictional film",[3] a position in which "the characters who perform direct address know more—or are in a position of greater knowledge within the fiction"[4] Of course, Hopper's 'greater knowledge' did not always lie within the fictional constraints of the films but broke free from the narrative. Thus the knowledge was of his own self-referral.

If we look over the collection of essays within this book, we find Dennis Hopper almost in a constant state of self-referral. He breaks not only the fourth wall in film but in almost every other medium. His photography work is embedded within the 1960s, the civil rights movements, the young stars of Hollywood. It becomes a definitive portrait of the era leading up to *Easy Rider*. In advertising and commercials, marketing strategists relied on consumer's familiarity with Hopper's past endeavours. The Ford Cougar commercial is the most blatant example, teaming a mature Hopper with *Easy Rider*'s Billy for a road trip. In music, Hopper was referenced by artists and musicians, and his soundtracks reflected the films' narratives. With his emotive and raw performances in *Mad Dog Morgan*, *White Star*, and *The Blackout*, he shatters the fourth wall into his own life. In Hopper's introduction to Viggo Mortensen's monograph *Recent Forgeries* (1998), he claims that "Art has a vanishing point... It transcends the artist's personal application and becomes yours."[5] From these essays, we discover that every aspect of Dennis Hopper's life was an experiment in constructing a truly inspired, transcendent, and artistic existence that now truly does belong to us.

Acknowledgements

This book started life in a very different way. Originally I had intended, by way of comparative essays, to examine ten forgotten or undervalued films of Dennis Hopper's career. The intended films were as follows: the quaint mid-life crisis movie *Carried Away,* the dark drama *The Blackout* directed by Abel Ferrara, cop thriller *Boiling Point,* low-budget noir *Out of Season,* the Australian film *The Night We Called it a Day* (in which Hopper played Frank Sinatra), the screwball *Search and Destroy,* the made-for-television sci-fi films *Space Truckers* and *Tycus,* Australian bush ranger bio *Dog Morgan*, and the German punk film *White Star.* My intention was to sit through these films and write about them immediately afterwards, throwing myself into the narrative as viewer and reviewer. I had all but written the book when I decided to incorporate all the facts and cultural points of interest that I had stumbled upon along the way—cultural footnotes that seemed relevant enough to the main text. I included sub-chapters that dealt with Hopper's artwork, his work in commercials and advertisements, his use of music to soundtrack his films, his relationship to the music industry, his involvement in American politics, and his influence on American popular culture. All this was to back up the gonzo-like narrative of the original book. Then I noticed something after reading an initial draft. To put it simply, I was not that interested in what I had written concerning the ten films. In some cases, the films had been forgotten or undervalued for a very good reason: for the most part, they were dreadful. *Space Truckers,* for example, has very few redeeming features, and the majority of the film's running time saw Hopper doing very little except standing around in his boxer shorts looking perplexed, whilst the zero-budget disaster movie *Tycus* offered cheap visual effects and stock footage from other films matched with some truly terrible dialogue delivery. These movies did not really need recovery. They were best left to the late-night cable channels for which some of them were made. What I began to find more interesting was the cultural footnotes—why indeed were they footnotes? When I began to research further, I found these aspects of Hopper's career deeply fascinating, incredibly contradictory, and bravely audacious. The comparison of ten films went out the window (for the most part anyway), and I drew my focus towards these aspects instead, something many books on Dennis Hopper promise to do but rarely deliver on. Some of the original book survives. The comparative essay on *The Blackout* and *Carried Away* revealed a great truth about Hopper's on-screen characters and their failures in love and emotional connections. The film *White Star* showed Hopper at his most raw and wild. It was a film that needed to be revaluated before Hopper's performance was lost to the ether. *White Star* was matched up in a comparative study with *Mad Dog Morgan*, but the main argument had already been made by *White Star's* bare-knuckle realism, so it too was dropped but has been published by the online literary magazine *Empty Mirror*. I do, however, regret the loss of *Search and Destroy*, a film so wacky that it was virtually impossible to transcribe the giddiness and dark humour of the film to a critique that could illustrate this excitement. I remember my good friend Andy Jury describing the film as "either the best film I've ever seen, or the worst", and I think I am still weighing up that conundrum. My thanks go to Andy, Dipesh Patel, Mariam Ashraf, and Hannah Lenagh-Snow for indulging me and allowing me to verbally contemplate the ideas that are found in this book. I would also like to thank Clare Hardy, Alfie Bown, Daniel Bristow, Alex Cox, John W. Whitehead, and Michael Khavari at *Gadfly Online*, and Denise Enck at *Empty Mirror*. Thanks to Mum and Dad, Joanne, Libby, Evie, Brian, Gail, Ross, Kara, Seamus, and Stanley. As always, I am eternally grateful to my wife Jamie and our son Hayden for their continuous support.

Notes

Introduction

1. *Duchamp, "The Creative Act", p. 77.*
2. Drazen, *On Blue Velvet*, p. 53.
3. Rombes, "The Blue Velvet Project", #58.
4. Hampton, "Impressions of an Existential Stunt Man".
5. Gilroy-Hirtz, *The Lost Album.*

Scenes from a Revolutionary Life

1. Merv Griffin Show, "Dennis Hopper Interview".
2. Bellamy, *American Dream*, p. 24.
3. Rodriguez, *A Madness to His Method,* p. 20.
4. Stanislavski, *An Actor Prepares,* p. 15.
5. Cole and Krich-Chinoy, *Actors on Acting*, p. 623.
6. Auster and Quart, *American Film and Society Since 1945*, p. 62.
7. Berardinelli, "Giant".
8. Dawson, *Dennis Hopper Interviews,* p. 130.
9. Diski, *The Sixties,* p. 5.
10. Manning, "Preface," p. 7.
11. Orléan, "Photography, Writing, Acting," p. 126.
12. Kalat," Night Tide".
13. Winkler, *Wild Ride of a Hollywood Rebel*, p. 65.
14. Dawson, *Dennis Hopper Interviews,* p. 161.
15. Winkler, *Wild Ride of a Hollywood Rebel*, p. 92.
16. Steppenwolf, "The Pusher".
17. Dylan, "It's Alright Ma (I'm Only Bleeding)".
18. *Backstory* 2 "Stewart Stern: Out of the Soul", p. 304.
19. Tracy, "(En)fin de Cinema: Andrew Tracy on the Last Movie".
20. Russell, *Vietnam War Movies*, p. 55.
21. Tacon, "Great Directors: Wim Wenders".
22. Thoret, "Dennis/Hopper or The Man Who Was Two and One", p. 64.
23. Hedges, *War is a Force that Gives Us Meaning*, pp. 5, 6.
24. Morgan, "When Piers Morgan met Dennis Hopper".
25. Dawson, *Dennis Hopper Interviews,* p. 123.
26. Rombes, "The Blue Velvet Project", p. 103.
27. Kelly, *Sean Penn: His Life and Times*, pp. 185, 186.
28. Maslin, "Police vs. Street Gangs in Hopper's 'Colors'".
29. Orléan, *Dennis Hopper and the New Hollywood*, p. 136.
30. Rabin, "The Hot Spot/Killing Me Softly".
31. Ibid.

32. Godfrey, "Farewell Dennis Hopper".
33. Winkler, *Wild Ride of a Hollywood Rebel*, p. 277.
34. Dawson, *Dennis Hopper Interviews,* p. 164.

Hip-Hopp

1. Hopper, "Encounter with Travellers: Hopper and Wenders".
2. Luck, "The Late Dennis Hopper on Nicholson, Newman, Dylan and Dean".
3. Goodwin, *Dancing in the Distraction Factory,* p. 8.
4. King and Coffin, "I Wasn't Born to Follow".
5. Wilkin, "Screaming Metaphysical Blues".
6. Young, "My My Hey Hey (Out of the Blue)".
7. Goodwin, *Dancing in the Distraction Factory,* p. 59.
8. Moltke and Williams, "A Mind is a Terrible Thing to Waste".
9. Ice T, "Colors".
10. Kristopherson, "The Pilgrim, Chapter 33".
11. Kipling, "If", p. 134.
12. Cash, "God's Gonna Cut you Down".
13. Soderburg, "Dennis Hopper, Soundtrack Savant: The Unacknowledged Music Savvy Behind *Easy Rider*, *Out of the Blue*, and *Colors*".

The Elephant in the Room

1. O'Hare, "(Dennis) Hopper Evolves from Rebel to Republican".
2. WENN, "Hopper keeps Bush Support under Wraps".
3. Auster and Quart, *American Film and Society Since 1945,* p. 137.
4. Ibid., p. 140.
5. Huffington Post, "Bush-Supporter Dennis Hopper switches his vote: 'I pray' Obama Wins".
6. O'Hare, "(Dennis) Hopper Evolves from Rebel to Republican".
7. Ibid.
8. Dickenson, *Hollywood's New Radicalism*, p. 16.
9. Auster and Quart, *American Film and Society Since 1945,* p. 164.
10. Stein, "The Dead Zones".
11. Lowenstein, "Fear Across the Disciplines", p. 154.
12. Ibid., p. 155.
13. Hollywood.com, "Dennis Hopper cut out of his own film".
14. Heath and Potter, *The Rebel Sell: Why the Culture Can't be Jammed*, p. 62.
15. Ibid., p. 63.
16. Linderman, *Dennis Hopper Interviews*, p. 88.

Love and Hate

1. Martin, "Stars in our Eyes", p. 3.
2. Ibid., p. 12.
3. Ibid, p. 11.
4. Hampton, "Impressions of an Existential Stunt Man", p. 41.
5. Holden, "Adults With Choices, And Sex Is the Big One".
6. Hopper and Wenders, "Encounters with Travellers: Dennis Hopper and Wim Wenders".

Commercial Breakdown

1. Shaw, "Celebs go Abroad".
2. Ibid.
3. Streetlight Films, "Making of Dennis Hopper Ford Cougar".
4. NIKE, "Stanley Speaks: NIKE Releases Hopper Super Bowl Speech".
5. Doyle, "Dennis Does Ameriprise 2006-2008".
6. [6] Ibid.
7. Garfield, "Ameriprise's Dennis Hopper Spot: Wrong Icon, Right Tone".
8. Ibid.
9. Ibid.
10. Trenholm, "We've had Enough of the Orange 'Gold Spot' Cinema Adverts".
11. Medina, "Tod's in Tinseltown".
12. Ibid.
13. Vans UK, "Vans Release Dennis Hopper Collection".

White Light/White Heat

1. Stanislavski, *An Actor's Handbook,* p. 159.
2. Acton, "White Star".
3. Ibid.
4. Morgan, "When Piers Morgan met Dennis Hopper".
5. Spectacle, "White Star".
6. Ibid.
7. The Sydney Morning Herald, "Downhill ride for Maria after her tango with Brando".

Double Standards

1. Gilroy-Hirtz, "The Lost Album", p. 24.
2. Fuchs and Sassen, *Dennis Hopper* (*A Keen Eye*), p. 10.
3. Eardog Productions, "Actor Dennis Hopper, On Art".
4. Ibid.

5. Ibid.
6. Hampton, "Impressions of an Existential Stunt Man".
7. Gilroy-Hirtz, "The Lost Album", p. 29.
8. Foreman, "Dennis Hopper: The Missing Years".
9. Gilroy-Hirtz, "The Lost Album", p. 27.
10. Ibid., p. 19.
11. Harcourt, "Dennis Hopper Sets the Standard".
12. Harris, "Dennis Hopper – Bucharest Nights".
13. Fuchs and Sassen, *Dennis Hopper* (*A Keen Eye*), p. 83.
14. Ibid., p. 81.
15. Ibid., p. 83.
16. Ibid., p. 82.
17. Ibid., p. 13.
18. Ibid., p. 82.

Coda

1. Luck, "A Reefer Runs Through It: The Making of *Easy Rider*".
2. Drazen, *On Blue Velvet*, p. 61.
3. Bloom, *Breaking the Fourth Wall: Direct Address in the Cimema*, p. 14.
4. Ibid. p. 14.
5. Hopper, "Introduction", p. 5.

Bibliography

Monographs and Articles

Auster, Albert, and Leonard Quart. *American Film and Society Since 1945*. Westport: Praeger, 1991.

Bellamy, Linda. *The American Dream: The 50's (Our American Century)*. New York: Time-Life Books, 2003.

Bloom, Tom. *Breaking the Fourth Wall: Direct Address in the Cinema*. Edinburgh: Edinburgh University Press, 2012.

Cole, Toby, and Helen Krich-Chinoy, eds. *Actors on Acting*. New York: Crown Publishers, 1970.

Dawson, Nick, ed. *Dennis Hopper Interviews*. Jackson: University Press of Mississippi, 2012.

Dickenson, Ben. *Hollywood's New Radicalism: War, Globalisation and the Movies from Reagan to George W. Bush*. London: I.B. Taurus, 2006.

Diski, Jenny. *The Sixties*. New York: Profile Books, 2010.

Duchamp, Marcel. "'The Creative Act' - Session on the Creative Act, Convention of the American Federation of Arts, Houston, Texas, April 1957", in *Marcel Duchamp* by Robert Lebel, pp. 77-78. New York: Grove Press, 1959.

Drazen, Charles. *On Blue Velvet*. London: Bloomsbury, 1998.

Fuchs, Rudi, and Jan Hein Sassen. *Dennis Hopper (A Keen Eye): Artist, Photographer, Filmmaker*. Rotterdam: NAi Publishers, 2001.

Gilroy-Hirtz, Petra. *The Lost Album*. London: Prestel, 2012.

Goodwin, Andrew. *The Distraction Factory*. Minneapolis: University of Minnesota Press, 1992.

Hampton, Howard. "Impressions of an Existential Stunt Man: Looking Back at Dennis Hopper." *Film Comment*, May/June 2013.

Heath, Joseph, and Andrew Potter. *The Rebel Sell: Why the Culture Can't be Jammed*. Toronto: HarperCollins, 2004.

Hedges, Chris. *War is a Force that Gives Us Meaning*. New York: Anchor Books, 2003.

Hopper, Dennis. Introduction to *Recent Forgeries*, by Viggo Mortensen. Culver City: Smart Art Books, 1998.

Kelly, Richard T. *Sean Penn: His Life and Times*. London: Faber and Faber, 2005.

Kipling, Rudyard. "If" in *Selected Poems*. London: Penguin Classics, 2001.

Lowenstein, Adam. "Living Dead: Fearful Attractions of Film" in *Fear Across the Disciplines*, edited by Jan Plamper and Benjamin Lazier. Pittsburgh: University of Pittsburgh Press, 2012.

Manning, Robert. "Preface: The Shattered Glass" in *The Vietnam Experience: Images of War*, edited by Julene Fischer, 7. Boston: Boston Publishing Company, 1981.

Martin, Adrian. "The Misleading Man: Dennis Hopper" in *Stars in Our Eyes: The Star Phenomenon in the Contemporary Era*, edited by Angela Ndalianis and Charlotte Henry, pp. 2-19. Westport: Preager, 2002.

Orléan, Matthieu. "Photoghaphy, Writing, Acting...Movie-making had Everything in One Package: Interview with Dennis Hopper", in *Dennis Hopper and the New Hollywood*. Translated by David Radzinowicz, pp. 125-127. Paris: Flammarion, 2009.

Rodriguez, Elena. *Dennis Hopper: A Madness to His Method*. New York: St Martin's Press, 1988.

Russell, Jamie. *Vietnam War Movies*. Harpenden: Pocket Essentials, 2002.

Shafrazi, Tony, ed. *Dennis Hopper: Photographs 1961-1967*. London: Taschen, 2009.

Stanislavski, Constantin. *An Actor Prepares*. Translated by Elizabeth Reynolds Hapgood. New York: Routledge, 2003.

—. *An Actor's Handbook: An Alphabetical Arrangement of Concise Statements on Aspects of Acting*. Edited and translated by Elizabeth Reynolds Hapgood. New York: Routledge, 2004.

Thoret, Jean-Baptiste. "Dennis/Hopper or The Man Who Was Two and One" in *Dennis Hopper and the New Hollywood*. Translated by David Radzinowicz, pp. 62-66. Paris: Flammarion, 2009.

Winkler, Peter, L. *Dennis Hopper: The Wild Ride of a Hollywood Rebel*. London: Robson Press, 2011.

Websites and Electronic Media

Acton, Sarah. "White Star", *Takeonecff.com*. Published 13 September 2013. Accessed 11 October 2014. http://www.takeonecff.com/2013/white-star

Berardinelli, James. "Giant", *Reelviews.com*. Published 2014. Accessed 5 February 2014. http://www.reelviews.net/php_review_template.php?identifier=1904

Doyle, Jack. "Dennis Does Ameriprise, 2006-2008", *PopHistoryDig.com*. Published 17 June 2008. Accessed 22 November 2014. http://www.pophistorydig.com/topics/dennis-hopper-2006-2008/

Eardog Productions. "Actor Dennis Hopper, On Art", YouTube Video, 4:16. Published 11 December 2007. http://www.youtube.com/watch?v=olZk4ABm_g8

Foreman, Lisa. "Dennis Hopper: The Missing Years", *Thedailybeast.com*. Published 25 June 2014. Accessed 11 October 2014. http://www.thedailybeast.com/articles/2014/06/25/dennis-hopper-the-missing-years.html

Garfield, Bob. "Ameriprise's Dennis Hopper Spot: Wrong Icon, Right Tone", *Adage.com*. Published 19 November 2006. Accessed 12 May 2013. http://adage.com/article/ad-review/ameriprise-s-dennis-hopper-spot-wrong-icon-tone/113362/

Godfrey, Alex. "Farewell Dennis Hopper", *Sabotagetimes.com*. Published 21 June 2011. Accessed 27 November 2014. http://sabotagetimes.com/tv/at-home-with-dennis-hopper/

Harcourt, Glen. "Dennis Hopper Sets the Standard", *Artillerymag.com*. Published 1 July 2014. Accessed 17 November 2014. http://artillerymag.com/dennis-hopper-sets-standard/

Harris, Peter. "Dennis Hopper - Bucharest Nights", *pjhstudios.com*. Published 2 August 2010. Accessed 8 September 2013. http://www.pjhstudios.com/blog/2010/08/02/dennis-hopper-bucharest-nights/

Holden, Stephen. "Adults With Choices, And Sex Is the Big One", *Nytimes.com*. Published 29 March 1996. Accessed 23 November 2014. http://www.nytimes.com/movie/review?res=9D0DE6DA1539F93AA15750C0A960958260

Hollywood.com. "Dennis Hopper cut out of his own film", Published 8 August 2008. Accessed 12 May 2012. http://www.hollywood.com/news/movies/5287975/dennis-hopper-cut-out-of-his-own-film

Hopper, Dennis, and Wim Wenders. "Encounters with Travellers: Dennis Hopper and Wim Wenders", *Europeanfilmacadamy.org*. Published 3 February 2003. Accessed 17 November 2014. http://www.europeanfilmacademy.org/Hopper-and-Wenders-Until-the-End-of-the-World.147.0.html

Huffington Post. "Bush Supporter Dennis Hopper switches his vote: 'I pray' Obama Wins", *huffingtonPost.com*. Published 14 October 2008. Accessed 3 May 2014. http://www.huffingtonpost.com/2008/10/14/bush-supporter-dennis-hop_n_134433.html

Kalat, David. "Night Tide", *Tcm.com*. Publication date unknown. Accessed 12 December 2013. http://www.tcm.com/this-month/article/332310|332312/Night-Tide.html

Luck, Richard. "A Reefer Runs Through It: The Making of *Easy Rider*", *Sabotagetimes.com*. Published 20 November 2013. Accessed 17 November 2014. http://sabotagetimes.com/reportage/a-reefer-runs-through-it-the-making-of-easy-rider/

—. "The Late Dennis Hopper on Nicholson, Newman, Dylan, and Dean", *Sabotagetimes.com*. Published 3 Feb 2014. Accessed 30 October 2014. http://sabotagetimes.com/reportage/dennis-hopper-on-nicholson-newman-dylan-and-dean/

Maslin, Janet. "Police vs. Street Gangs In Hopper's 'Colors'", *Nytimes.com*. Published 15 April 1988. Accessed 4 November 2014. http://www.nytimes.com/movie/review?res=940DE3DD 1731F936A25757C0A96E948260

Medina, Marcy. "Tod's in Tinseltown", *Wmagazine.com*. Published 1 August 2008. Accessed 7 July 2014. http://www.wmagazine.com/fashion/accessories/2008/08/tods/

Merv Griffin Show. "Dennis Hopper Interview- Easy Rider/The Last Movie (Merv Griffin Show 1971)", YouTube Video, 10:05. Published 7 November 2012. Accessed 6 June 2013. http://www.youtube.com/watch?v=gcywX-IlWhE

McGilligan, Patrick. *Backstory 2: Interviews with Screenwriters of the 1940s and 1950s*. "Stewart Stern: Out of the Soul", Berkeley: University of California Press, c.1991. Accessed 27 October 2014. http://ark.cdlib.org/ark:/13030/ft0z09n7m0/

Morgan, Piers. "When Piers Morgan met Dennis Hopper", *GQ-magazine.co.uk*. Published 26 May 2010. Accessed 21 June 2013. http://www.gq-magazine.co.uk/entertainment/articles/2010-05/26/gq-film-piers-morgan-meets-dennis-hopper/page/2

NIKE. "Stanley Speaks - NIKE Releases Hopper Super Bowl Speech", *Sportsbusinessdaily.com*. Published 26 January 1995. Accessed 24 August 2014. http://www.sportsbusinessdaily.com/Daily/Issues/1995/01/26/Sponsorships-Advertising-Marketing/STANLEY-SPEAKS-NIKE-RELEASES-HOPPER-SUPER-BOWL-SPEECH.aspx

O'Hare, Kate. "(Dennis) Hopper Evolves from Rebel to Republican", *Freerepublic.com*. Published 26 October 2005. Accessed 3 June 2014. http://www.freerepublic.com/focus/chat/1510435/posts

Rabin, Nathan. "The Hot Spot/Killing Me Softly", *Thedissolve.com*. Published 13 August 2013. Accessed 6 November 2014. http://thedissolve.com/reviews/126-the-hot-spot-killing-me-softly/

Rombes, Nicholas. "The *Blue Velvet* Project, #58", *Filmmakermagazine.com*. Published 23 Dec 2011. Accessed 29 June 2014. http://filmmakermagazine.com/36631-the-blue-velvet-proect-58/#.U8a3kLGFitc

Shaw, Jessica. "Celebs going Abroad", *Entertainmentweekly.com*. Published 15 November 1996. Accessed 24 August 2014. http://www.ew.com/ew/article/0,,295018,00.html

Soderberg, Brandon. "Dennis Hopper, Soundtrack Savant: The Unacknowledged Music Savvy Behind *Easy Rider, Out of the Blue*, and *Colors*", *Villagevoice.com*. Published 1 June 2011. Accessed 13 November 2014. http://blogs.villagevoice.com/music/2010/06/dennis hopper s.php

Spectacle. "White Star", *spectacletheater.com*. Accessed 5 May 2013. http://www.spectacletheater.com/white-star/

Stein, Elliot. "The Dead Zones", *Villagevoice.com*. Published 7 January 2003. Accessed 25 November 2014. http://www.villagevoice.com/2003-01-07/film/the-dead-zones/

Streetlight Films. "The Making of Dennis Hopper Ford Cougar". Published 20 June 2013. Accessed 22 November 2014. http://vimeo.com/68806977

Sydney Morning Herald. "Downhill ride for Maria after her Tango with Brando". Published 22 June 2006. Originally published in London Telegraph, date unknown. Accessed 18 July 2013. http://www.smh.com.au/news/film/downhill-ride-for-maria-after-her-tango-with-brando/2006/06/21/1150845244689.html

Tacon, David. "Great Directors: Wim Wenders", *Sensesofcinema.com*. Published 26 May 2003. Accessed 4 March 2013. http://sensesofcinema.com/2003/great-directors/wenders/

Tracy, Andrew. "(En)fin de Cinema: Andrew Tracy on the Last Movie", *Reverseshot.com*. Autumn 2004. Accessed 2 February 2014. http://www.reverseshot.com/legacy/autumn04/lastmovie.html

Trenholm, Rich. "We've had Enough of the Orange 'Gold Spot' Cinema Adverts", *Cnet.com*. Published 8 November 2010. Accessed 23 November 2014. http://www.cnet.com/news/weve-had-enough-of-the-orange-gold-spot-cinema-adverts/

Vans UK. "Vans Release Dennis Hopper Collection", Published 7 May 2011. Accessed 12 June 2013. http://www.vans.co.uk/news/item/7078/vans-release-dennis-hopper-collection

WENN. "Hopper keeps Bush Support under Wraps", *Contact Music*. Published 7 September 2005. Accessed 2 May 2014. http://www.contactmusic.com/news-article/hopper-keeps-bush-support-under-wraps

Discography

Cash, Johnny. "Johnny Cash - 'God's Gonna Cut you Down' (2006)", YouTube, 2:49. Published 1 November 2009. Accessed 3 October 2013.

Dylan, Bob. "'It's Alright Ma (I'm Only Bleeding)' - Bob Dylan (5/7/65) Bootleg", YouTube, 8:09. Published 11 August 2013. Accessed 24 September 2013.

Ice T. "Colors", (1988) YouTube, 3:59. Published 17 May 2013. Accessed 7 November 2014.

King, Carole. "I Wasn't Born to Follow", YouTube, 3:45. Published 5 June 2011. Accessed 7 October 2014.

Kristofferson, Kris. "'The Pilgrim, Chapter 33' (Live)", YouTube, 5:32. Published 7 August 2011. Accessed 29 October 2013.

Moltke, Shawn and Marlon Williams. "A Mind is a Terrible Thing to Waste", YouTube, 4:30. Published June 30 2014. Accessed 13 November 2014.

Steppenwolf. "Steppenwolf - 'The Pusher' - Live at the Matrix San Francisco 1966", YouTube, 10:43. Published 18 December 2010. Accessed 5 October 2013.

Wilkin, John Buck. "Screaming Metaphysical Blues", YouTube, 2:07. Published 22 October 2013. Accessed 5 November 2013.

Young, Neil. "My My Hey Hey (Out of the Blue)", YouTube, 3:51. Published 7 November 2011. Accessed 22 June 2014.